resurrection monday

the true story of a death to life experience

nancy and chris conant

Resurrection Monday: The True Story of a Death to Life Experience

© 2013 by Nancy and Chris Conant
Genre: Christian Autobiography

Publisher: Heyoo House
Printed/Electronic Distribution: Amazon
ISBN: 978-0-9885403-0-9

Language: English
Cover Design by More Cabbage LLC, Chris Conant

Note to reader: Some of the names in this book have been changed to protect the privacy of the individuals mentioned. Also, much of the dialogue between Chris and Nancy has been reconstructed from memory during a chaotic time. Nevertheless, the eyewitness accounts are truthful and accurately depict the circumstances surrounding Resurrection Monday.

Media Contact and Speaking Inquiries: Chris Conant, la@morecabbage.com

This book is dedicated to our families, whom we deeply love and to our sister Sandy, who we miss more than words can express. Can't wait to see you on the other side, Sis…

Contents

Foreword

BY PASTOR OLEN GRIFFING

Watching this story unfold was at times really wonderful and yet at other times painful. This is an adventure in which Chris and Nancy were graced to walk through together. I was gripped by the fact that two people whose lives are dedicated to a covenant relationship could not only endure, but could come through trying circumstances overwhelmingly victorious.

I was impressed to see two very successful people, Chris who possesses fantastically deep dimensions of entrepreneurial creativity and Nancy who has a very moving passion for expressing God's beauty through art, be so open and transparent in sharing their life experiences. There is no doubt this book will be life and freedom to all hungry souls who imbibe.

I got so emotionally involved in this story that I could hardly wait to discover what would unfold from one chapter to the next. It has been exciting to learn of the victories that have been experienced in Chris and Nancy's and their children's lives after going through such tragic circumstances. This book makes one want to shout "Hallelujah" to the faithfulness of God.

Chris and Nancy integrate life-tested precepts giving practical application for each reader no matter what one's situation may be. Each thought in this book is pregnant with insight. The reading of this book is user-friendly. It will greatly encourage everyone who has struggled in life or that knows someone who has or is struggling. What hope it brings!

We can't live a significant life in our own strength, but Jesus Christ can and will through you if you will simply believe this "Good News." The truth in this book will bring increase in your life and show what the devil has meant for harm, God will go to great lengths to turn it for your good.

I heartily recommend this book to you knowing that it will increase your faith to the glory of God.

Pastor Olen Griffing
Founder Shady Grove Church, Grand Prairie, TX
International Director, AOI Network of Churches and
Ministries, Grand Prairie, TX

Preface

BY NANCY CONANT

This book chronicles my battle with Multiple Sclerosis as well as the events that took place on Easter Sunday of 2009, the following Monday and the days and weeks that followed. I consider that Monday a day of rebirth. This will be better understood later in the book.

I feel compelled to let the reader in on my journey, not because of any great accomplishment that I've achieved, but rather, by sharing in my failures, I hope to shed light on the potholes along the road of life so that I may help others to avoid them. In other words, I want others to learn from my mistakes and more importantly, allow others to witness how far God is willing to go to save a life.

I hope the words in this book will reveal the truth about God's grace for everyone. Grace from God is simply His favor to succeed. He carries the struggling believer through the deepest valley only to emerge on the other side victorious and in my case, alive.

I have taken an unconventional approach in writing this book: I invited my husband, Chris, to write it with me. You will surely hear the difference in our "voices" as well as our experiences.

The important thing is that in every way, whether from false motives or true, Christ is preached. And because of this I rejoice. Yes, and I will continue to rejoice, for I know that through your prayers and God's provision of the Spirit of Jesus Christ what has happened to me will turn out for my deliverance. I eagerly expect and hope that I will in no way be ashamed, but will have sufficient courage so that now as always Christ will be exalted in my body, whether by life or by death. For to me, to live is Christ and to die is gain. If I am to go on living in the body, this will mean fruitful labor for me. Yet what shall I choose? I do not know! I am torn between the two: I desire to depart and be with Christ, which is better by far; but it is more necessary for you that I remain in the body. Convinced of this, I know that I will remain, and I will continue with all of you for your progress and joy in the faith, so that through my being with you again your boasting in Christ Jesus will abound on account of me.

Philippians 1:18 - 26 New International Version (NIV)

Nancy Conant
nancyconant.com
Dallas, TX
April 13, 2013

Acknowledgements

Only God can take a tragedy and turn it into triumph. We want to begin by giving thanks first and foremost to Him who is able to do abundantly more than we could ever ask or hope for – Jesus Christ.

Thank you, to our many dear and faithful friends, Bob and Anna Oliver, Heather Harbaugh, Linda Hausermann, Joan Blinn, Shayla Anderson, Michelle Hlavac, and Paula Sterns. Thank you for coming alongside, riding our kids around, bringing over a meal and praying for us every step of the way.

Thank you to our dear friend, Linda Agnew who gave us strength and support during hard times. Thank you for being a part of our business at More Cabbage.

We want to extend a perpetual thank you to Joani Dockery who, still with us at More Cabbage, is the right person at the right time in our lives. Consistently you have been faithful, discreet, prayerful and a true servant of the Living God. Your ministry to our family is overwhelming. Your stories are always welcome! Your crowns await you in heaven! Thank you also for lending us your editing skills during the process of producing this book.

Thanks be to God, for planting us among healthy, mature, church families who live out the Word of God at:

Valley Vineyard Christian Fellowship, Reseda, CA (1984-2006) Pastors Bill Dwyer and Lynn Cory. Lynn, thank you for your invaluable input. Thank you also to you and Jo for your warm hospitality. You always make us feel we have family to return to. We love you.

Grace Vineyard Christian Fellowship, Arlington, TX (2006-2011) Pastor Bob and Anna Oliver

Gateway Church – Grand Prairie Campus, Grand Prairie, TX (2011- current) Pastors Robert Morris, Mark Jobe and Josh Briscoe

We want to thank the following friends and family for making contributions to our lives and this book: Paul Jones, Heather Harbaugh, Crista Darr, Tami McNulty, Sally O'Connor, Jan Enright, Solica Griffith, Daniel Miller, Jim and Sandy Conant, Sandy Summers and Carol Amante. By the way, Sal, thank you for allowing me to share your gift of music with others.

A very relieving thanks to Pat Nolan and the committee and supporters of the Dream Fund in Dallas, TX who miraculously covered our medical expenses.

A huge thank you to the National Multiple Sclerosis Society of Los Angeles and North Texas who supplied us our wheelchair and the family retreats that refresh us.

Many thanks to Pastor Olen Griffing for writing the forward to this book and to Lynn Cory, Rhett Smith, Michael O'Connor and Brian Sumner for sharing your thoughts about our book and getting behind this project.

Thank you Rebekah and Meghan for your love. We love you right back.

Finally, to all of you who have believed God's best for us and supported our family—you know who you are—and for fighting this battle with us on your knees; thank you from the bottom of our hearts.

CHAPTER 01

A Task I Wouldn't Wish on Anyone
BY CHRIS

2:30 AM, Monday, April 13, 2009

It's late and I'm in my home office, upstairs in the back corner of the house. The office is a long, converted add-on space, so the walls feel tight and narrow. There is a window to my left. I peer out into the dark night, fixing my tired stare on the empty space in front of the house where a cop car was parked just minutes before. I turn back to my desk, where my laptop sits open to a browser window.

I'm online looking at the county morgue to see if my wife's name is there - a task I wouldn't wish on anyone. There is a public list of new arrivals that is updated about every hour. I check the Tarrant County morgue and go to the C's. No Nancy Conant.

I force the panic swelling in my throat into a downward swallow, pushing the threat into my chest. I check the neighboring Dallas

County morgue web site. No Nancy.

I search hotels local to our house. There are four of them within ten miles. I start calling. Each call ends with, "I'm sorry, there's no guest registered by that name." I can't find her.

I picture our SUV stuck nose down in Joe Pool lake, mostly submerged and filling quickly with water, its skid marks veering off the road in a right curve over bushes and mowing a cluster of mesquite trees. It carves a path through the brush and down a steep embankment. Nancy is trapped inside slapping the driver's side windows with both hands. Large branches lie broken encumbering the rescue.

No. My subconscious stops that scene from playing out in my mind. Then I think to call a couple of local hospitals. Not there either. She isn't listed as a patient.

I realize that I have business presentations in a few hours to two clients, and they're important. One of them was scheduled three weeks ago. I am forced to decide to send an email to both clients, apologizing that I have to postpone because of a family emergency. I send it just before 2:50 AM. At the same time, a new thought grabs me. I realize the girls don't have school this day. It's a free day, which means that I have to be available to them when they wake up and then all day – or find them a place to go.

What would I say to the girls when they woke up? Should I tell them I thought Mom decided to spend the night in a hotel and I didn't know where she was because we hadn't spoken since before church?

Even though I knew her voicemail would pick up, I dial Nancy's cell phone again for the seventh time. I just want to hear her voice.

"Hi, this is Nancy. I'm sorry I missed you. Please leave a message and I'll call you back."

I miss her.

I check the morgues again for both counties. When I brought up the Dallas County morgue an update had been posted. A new arrival. Jane Doe.

A sinking feeling hit me, *this could be her,* I thought. If Nancy was without identification, it's possible the morgue wouldn't know who she is. *How do I find out? Do I want to find out?* As I click on the link that offered a brief description, I hold my breath. Female. 70s. Gray hair. I breathe out all the air in my lungs in relief. Nancy was in her 40's with dark brown hair.

I picture the drawers at the morgue. I think about how I don't know what they're called—the refrigerated ones with the bodies in them. My eyes feel heavy so I close them. I put my hands over

3

my face and rest my elbows on my desk.

My head falls forward into slumber, almost falling asleep at my laptop. In one second, I shake my head from the sensation of nodding off. With total consciousness I pull out a short but meaningful prayer from deep within:

"Lord, sustain her life. Keep her alive. Let someone find her," I said aloud.

Then I stand up, walk downstairs to our bedroom, and crash into bed.

CHAPTER 02

Five Weeks Earlier
BY CHRIS

"We're out of fuel and I need to land." I looked directly at my co-pilot, Nancy Conant. My wife.

We were flying in a single-engine seaplane in Central America, and I had to look for water. In the clearing below I saw a small pond beneath a canopy of rainforest trees. It was just large enough that I could drop the plane down and manage an emergency landing.

I was relieved that there were no other passengers, like our girls, Rebekah and Meghan. I recall thinking that if *we* didn't make it, I hoped they would be able to carry on without us. They were young: twelve and ten, and the idea that they would be under the care of others unnerved me.

I dropped the plane down in East Belize. We were coming in high, so a quick nose dive followed by a sharp pull on the stick put us a few feet above the water. I gently eased it down.

The spray from the water brushed by the twin pontoons. I glanced at Nancy, who had both hands against the instrument panel, bracing herself from flying forward on impact.

In the cockpit, we had all this stuff at our feet. It looked like a car that hadn't been cleaned out in months. I briefly considered, "How did we create such a mess?" The pontoons made a loud hum as I set the plane into the pond. It coasted on the water for a couple hundred yards then, running out of "runway," I made a u-turn and used some thrust to the plane's prop to pull us to the beachfront. I cut the power to the engine and brought the plane to rest.

I wondered why this was happening to us. Maybe it was the fact that I hadn't prepared with enough fuel, or maybe we were too weighted down with stuff. I had never, ever thought I would have to make an emergency landing in a plane. Perhaps God was trying to get my attention.

I looked out the window, and I could see the bottom of the pond. It seemed to be only waist-deep. As I gazed out to the left, an ancient, ten-story, Aztec-looking tower stood tall enough that I had to crane my neck to see its upper reach. It was uninhabited, but it seemed like it had been erected long ago as a pyramid-shaped temple of some sort for an ancient deity like Quetzalcoatl.

Out the right window I noticed a gently sloping clearing in the rainforest that seemed to go on for a mile. It was as if the clearing served as the route that the locals would use to walk to this monumental structure. It rained year round, so the grass was green and the foliage bordering the clearing was thick. Jurassic Park-sized leaves lopped over from the margin onto the clearing.

Then it dawned on me. This wasn't a small pond. It was a reflecting pool, designed to impress the splendor of this man-made structure on its worshipers.

I turned to look at Nancy.

"Are you alright?" I asked.

She looked up and with a faint breath said, "Yeah, I'm okay."

I pulled the door handle and jumped out the pilot's door into the waist-deep water with a small splash. I started to push the plane toward the shore, just 30 feet away. It was heavy, but on water, it moved slowly to the shore.

Then I saw people.

As I walked up the beach and drew closer I was relieved when I was greeted by familiar faces. Camped out near the shore were people we knew from our church. Paul Jones was first to approach.

Paul is a very quick-witted, dependable, hard-working guy with a big heart for God. No one can out-serve Paul. I've discovered that, in addition to sowing his time and resources into people, he is also very practical. He is handy with all sorts of projects—whether construction or outdoor adventure or coordinating a group, I can almost always say "Paul's your man."

It was no surprise that Paul came up and said, "Hey, man, that was a pretty tight parking spot. You okay?"

"Yeah," I chuckled, as if it were no big deal. I had some travel gear hanging over my shoulder, so I leaned it down against a palm tree.

He quickly changed the subject, "Hey, do you have a wrench?"

"No. No, I don't," I said regretfully. I was at a loss. I am usually so prepared.

Just then Heather Harbaugh came over. Heather is married to Lee, and they have six homeschooled children. Heather's parents are Christians, and I would suspect, knowing Heather, that it doesn't stop there. I bet there is a legacy of prayer through generations of Christians in her past.

I would describe Heather as a sweet friend to whom God has given His cell number. You know what I mean? As if she has direct access to the inner chamber of God's throne room. The Father is talking with Jesus about some heavenly to-do, when suddenly His phone's ringtone, "Holy, Holy, Holy," goes off. "Hang on, Jesus. It's Heather. I need to take this call."

Heather walks every day in power and authority by understanding her identity is *in* Christ. This, I think, is the major difference between people who describe themselves as Christians (like an adjective) and those who call themselves Christian (the noun). Christians (the nouns) are living their lives in Christ to fullness: because knowing who you are *in* Christ changes everything. It changes your perspective, your faith, your understanding of God's power to overcome, your ability to see God's way out; it changes your life experience, and you can have powerful, effective prayers and experience healings while in Christ.

Heather is *in* Christ.

She walked up right after Paul shot his question to me and, with perfect timing, interjected, "I have some tools."

I looked at her outstretched hands. There were four different wrench-like tools, each one with a different, brightly colored handle. They were shiny and new.

Out of nowhere the sound of seagulls and ocean waves crashing on a beach filled my ears.

It was my alarm clock. Instead of harsh tones or a radio station, I prefer the California sounds to nudge me out of my slumber.

It was March 11, 2009 when I awoke from my dream. It was 6:30 am to be exact. I had no idea at the time what the significance of this dream was. *So much symbolism, what did it all mean?* I didn't know. It was like I just drove past a road sign warning me of our travel ahead, but it didn't seem to register what I was supposed to do.

I had to make sure the girls were up and getting ready for school, so I put my feet on the floor and started my day.

CHAPTER 03

The Pronouncement
BY NANCY

Like most people living in Los Angeles, I ran on the fast track of life: being a wife, a mom, a daughter and sister in a big Italian family; a co-owner and CEO of a growing marketing company; working a full schedule from sunup to sundown…sitting in traffic to get anywhere.

It was April of 2004. We were busily preparing for a client's upcoming marketing event, to be held in Arizona. The ramp-up time to the show was insane. We were working long days and into the evenings.

I noticed something was not quite right with my peripheral vision.

I decided to tell Chris about it.

"Chris, when I'm driving and making a right turn or backing up, I can't see."

"What do you mean, you can't see?" Chris investigated.

"I mean, it's like I have a blind spot—I see nothing—actually," I told him. "When I try to look to the side, I have to turn my head completely like this." I rotated my head as far as it could turn while keeping my torso still.

"My peripheral vision isn't there."

Chris got quiet. He seemed to lack compassion when it came to all things pertaining to ill-health, which is probably why he decided to change his major in college from Pre-Med to Communications.

At the time we had two cars; one owned outright we called Stork, because it was a minivan that delivered our seven and five year-old daughters from here to there. The other was a leased vehicle, named Bullet, because it was silver, aerodynamic and fast.

"I think you should drive Stork 'cause Bullet is leased," Chris was still being uncompassionate but practical, "I mean, just in case you were to crash, Bullet might be costly to repair."

Looking back now, it still shocks me that we thought the suggestion was reasonable instead of *insane,* but this is an example of our thinking at the time: Just keep on going – no matter what. Don't stop for anything!

When I went in to see my primary care physician, Dr. Braunstein, I announced my order.

"I'm a race car and you're my pit crew. Fix me up and get me back on the track – quick!"

Dr. Braunstein had a solemn look on his face when he replied, "Not with this one, Nancy. This is not some simple cold. I'm afraid to say this one is big, and you need to be seen by a neurologist right away."

While Chris was in Arizona to press on with the marketing event, I was lying in the neurologist's office getting a spinal tap. After a battery of lengthy and painful tests, the doctor confirmed what my primary care physician feared.

I had Multiple Sclerosis.

By the time Chris returned from his business trip, my vision diminished to a spinning pinhole. There was complete darkness that seemed to circulate around the tiniest bit of light.

I was rendered 90% blind.

All I could do was lay on the couch with my eyes closed. I couldn't manage to be there for the girls. I couldn't cook. I could barely dial a phone. *What is going on, God?*

As I laid there, I didn't know what to do with myself or how to be there for my family. My mind was swirling. *How are we going to live like this?*

I started a game of the "what ifs." *What if this Multiple Sclerosis causes me to lose my sight permanently? What if I lose the use of my hands or legs? What if I can't care for my husband and children? What if I wind up in a wheelchair? What if we have to sell our two-story home and move into a one-story?*

Chris was already on overload between work and picking up all the slack that was apparently slipping away from me. *What if we each didn't pull our own weight? How would we be able to make it? What if this...? And what if that...? What will become of us?!*

Oh, the range of emotions poured over me like crashing waves. Feelings of desperate fear to outright rage and everything in between engulfed me. This was an injustice of major proportions! How could this be happening to me?! Then I sank into a deep depression and threw the biggest pity party I could ever invite myself to. Little did I know that this attitude and outlook drained me of whatever strength I had left.

I just spiraled deeper into depression.

It wasn't the first time.

I've had an ongoing battle with depression most of my life, but this was at a whole new level. Long ago, the Lord freed me from the chains of pain, loneliness, self-pity, anger and rage that led me into places I refer to as the "dark night of the soul." They were places of torment. They were places of isolation and all sorts of addiction, places of despondency and death. Certainly He had delivered me out of those snares for good, right?

Early on in my relationship with God I had been healed from wounds of a tumultuous childhood and a wildly promiscuous young adulthood.

When I was young, I had a deep-seated aversion to authority. The youngest of six, I never had my say and have many memories of being put down and overlooked. I remember being told by family members that I was not allowed to touch the TV – at 17. Other messages were stated loud and clear: that I was stupid. That I would never amount to anything. That I was nothing but a quitter. That I was ugly. That everyone would be better off without me. These were the words that I heard that defined who I was.

My way of dealing with it was to retreat and turn the feelings against myself while I also lashed out in rage and blamed everyone else for my problems. I spent long hours isolated in my room, consumed with anger, plotting to escape from my parents and siblings.

I escaped all right. I discovered drugs early in the fourth grade. I

15

was high on something most of my school years and can't remember much of my childhood. I started hanging out with the wrong crowd finding myself at friends' houses whose parents rolled marijuana joints for us!

When boys entered the picture, they became a substitute for the love, attention and acceptance that I needed and craved. Meanwhile, the rage inside burned all the more. I made choices to fill the hurt in my heart with the empty solace of promiscuity and really harmful, unhealthy relationships. It wasn't love. I was just trying to fill a void.

The culmination of these life choices created a big depression soup, where everything was mixed together and my reactions were always tied to more than just the emotions of the moment. It was always everyone else's fault. I was a mess before the Lord got hold of me!

Many years later, in my twenties, I dealt honestly with these issues. A friend introduced me to some Bible verses and this one stood out:

Come let us reason together says the Lord. Though your sins are like scarlet, they will be white as snow; though they are red like crimson, they shall be [white] as wool.

Isaiah 1:18 New King James Version (NKJV)

This was a deal I couldn't pass up, so I traded with God: my depression for His joy. I came to realize that the same forgiveness God extends to me is mine to extend to others. The behaviors to temporarily escape from life were dealt with, honestly, through Godly counsel. I had a breakthrough with my depression as well as the many areas of bondage that had hold of me.

I truly believed I had lifelong victory, immunity even, over the grip of these vices once and for all. I had been totally healed and transformed from all this past stuff. So why – how – could I find myself with MS and in the depths of despair once again, facing a heaviness and darkness I thought was dealt with long ago?

"When an impure spirit comes out of a person, it goes through arid places seeking rest and does not find it. Then it says, 'I will return to the house I left.' When it arrives, it finds the house swept clean and put in order. Then it goes and takes seven other spirits more wicked than itself, and they go in and live there. And the final condition of that person is worse than the first."

Luke 11:24-26 New International Version (NIV)

CHAPTER 04

This is Bad!

BY CHRIS

Something wasn't quite right with Nancy. It began with some simple balance trouble and fatigue. At first I just thought it was "normal, after-workout" de-stress. We had always been an active couple, so I didn't really know how to respond at first when she told me she was feeling this way. There was nothing I could do. I couldn't fix it.

Eventually, signs of memory loss and major peripheral vision impairment showed up. This really scared me. We didn't quite know what was happening until a neurologist in Los Angeles diagnosed Nancy with MS.

The news hit me hard.

He told us, "Multiple Sclerosis is when your immune system begins to attack the myelin sheath, which is the protective coating around your nerves. As this irreparable process continues, the nerves become damaged and this subsequently causes all kinds of motor skill, muscle and nerve impairments, such as what's happening to the optic nerve, affecting peripheral vision." He continued, "People with MS experience extreme fatigue, may lose balance and, over time, require the aid of a wheelchair. Everyone who has MS reacts differently to the disease. For some, it may affect brain function. Others might have trouble walking. Some days you might feel okay; other days might be 'down' physical days, which could fuel emotions like depression or anger."

Wait. Wheelchair? Brain function? This is bad!

We immediately sought out physicians for second opinions and chased a few options for Nancy. It all seemed to confirm that MS was not only Nancy's diagnosis, but also a diagnosis for me, too. I remember thinking, *our life is going to be really different around here.*

We, of course, studied up on all the latest MS treatments. These are called disease-modifying drugs, as there is no actual cure for this disease to date. The National Multiple Sclerosis Society was helpful to us during this discovery process, by providing assistance with our research.

We began a year of investigating several different MS medications – all self-injectable. Over time, Nancy tried all five treatments available on the market. Some were daily subcutaneous injections with short needles; one treatment was administered intramuscularly through a long needle. Nancy couldn't give herself that shot; I had to play nurse.

The problem with each one of these drugs was the very serious side effects, the least of which gave Nancy flu-like symptoms for three out of seven days a week. Others caused "site reactions" where her skin would break out in hives with each shot. She was miserable. It was hard to watch her struggle through this. It wasn't even close to "quality of life."

During this time and since her diagnosis we spared no expense seeking cures or relief through other means: holistic, supplemental, organic and nutritional. We heard dental fillings with mercury were bad for MS patients. Nancy had them replaced. Nancy tried many supplements from multi-level marketing companies and whole food distributors. We investigated bee pollen. European studies. We switched our diet to organic. Everyone had advice. We went down a lot of rabbit trails. It's hard to determine what, if any, helped.

As much as I could figure, since there is no cure for MS, that first neurologist pronounced a death sentence over Nancy. His words were powerful. I trusted them. Then I entered a period of denial and insensitivity, focused mostly on finding solutions that modern medicine or nutritional science would correct. As if some miracle pill would make it all go away.

At the same time, I love my wife and I want the best for her. I knew a complete healing from God was the best possible outcome. I set out to pray for healing, not consistently, but definitely enough that God heard me repeat it – sometimes asking for, begging for, and declaring a healing. Sometimes I would ask out loud and sometimes under my breath. Usually I was demanding, like in a battle, claiming my rights as a Christian to a total MS healing through Jesus over Nancy. At other times I simply prayed for a symptom removal, or just, grace.

CHAPTER 05

Weakness

BY NANCY

I was incredibly relieved when my vision was restored after several weeks of prayer. At first an intensive steroid infusion treatment hardly worked, so we asked those faithful to the task to continue to pray for us. Next, I started a course of oral steroids, and it was during that time that my vision began to return and I eventually could see again. I was thanking God that there was a way through it.

I was dealing with my first Multiple Sclerosis flare-up, called an exacerbation. I experienced this flare-up on my optic nerves. Up until that point, it was the longest, most frightening month of my life.

MS is one scary disease. This disease has taken me through many hills and valleys. I can best describe it like there's a ticking time bomb living within me that could go off at any moment.

There are several types of MS. The type I was diagnosed with is the most common disease course, labeled Relapse-Remitting MS (RRMS). According to the National Multiple Sclerosis Society, a person with RRMS experiences attacks (also called relapses or exacerbations) of worsening neurologic function, followed by periods of remission in which partial or complete recovery occurs.

This simply means that one day I may look and feel fine, and the next day I neither look nor feel fine. It affects me wherever my nerves touch, which of course, is everywhere in my body. Today it could be a headache combined with pins and needles in my right leg. Tomorrow it may be the same or nothing at all. The next day I might feel paralysis on the entire left side of my body. Without warning, and lasting for an unknown period of time, I could be in the middle of experiencing exacerbations, followed by a period of time where I might be free from symptoms.

This is a progressive illness. Effects from previous exacerbations can and have remained, such as being unsteady. I started feeling off-balance during an exacerbation and many years later it remains and results in frequent falls.

I simply don't know when MS is going to strike, how it will manifest itself and if it will become permanent. Because MS can strike anywhere the nervous system reaches, it affects each person in various ways.

True to the diagnosis, sometimes I feel and look fine. As a matter of fact, many MS patients hear this "compliment" often: *"You tell me you have MS, but you look so good!"*

There is actually an MS support group named "But You Look So Good," poking fun at the frustration of knowing the average Joe doesn't understand what an MS patient is going through *inside* their body.

At other times I struggle with debilitating fatigue that is so intense it forces me to rest several times a day. Then, without warning, parts of my body just stop functioning, as they should: legs, arms, hands, bladder, bowels, cognition, speech, balance, energy (just to name a few). I can suffer anything from irritating tingling, to disruptive spasms, to complete malfunction. And then sometimes, those areas seem to be getting better while other malfunctions have become permanent. It is a confusing, progressive illness, which as of yet has no cure.

One of the many devastating effects of MS is weakness. It's a kind of weakness that takes me out of the game – completely. This weakness prevents me from functioning or doing the simplest of tasks. It is so heavy at times that I am forced into a wheelchair.

I've learned that it is easy to take for granted *doing* the basic things in life. I'm talking about taking a shower, getting to a bathroom (on time!), cooking a meal for my family, going to pick something up from the store or playing with my kids.

I joke about the commonly used phrases: "Oh, I'll just run in…" or "I'll just zip over there…" Truth be told, I don't *run* or *zip* anytime or anywhere anymore. Reality is that I hobble and fall and take much too much time to do the simplest of tasks such as getting dressed. Because I am unable to lift my legs, putting on pants takes me minutes rather than seconds. If I'm not careful to sit down, this activity could involve a fall. (Think cow tipping). It's almost funny – if it weren't so pathetic.

You name it, and doing most anything makes me weak. The reach of MS is far and wide, and every area in my life has been touched by it. *If* I manage to, say, take a shower, I could have to lie down for an hour to refuel for the next task, like going to the kitchen for a bowl of cereal! I struggle to find the words to describe the frustration that results from being stripped of the ability to "do," especially when compared to the active lifestyle I leave behind.

I began to question God. *Why would You allow this to happen? I have things to do! You have plans for me! What will the future hold for me? For my family?* I felt like I was gazing into nothing – an empty future completely void of any hope. It was easy to convince myself I was becoming completely useless.

The truer reality is that I listened to Satan, who is described in the Bible as a liar and the father of lies. He's not just a little red dude on my shoulder with a pitchfork whispering into my ear. His lies were actually influencing my thought life. I began to hear in my mind, and believe: *You can't do anything. You're a burden to others. People can't understand what you're going through. They think you're faking it.* These lies were piercing like fiery arrows straight to the heart. They were changing my outlook on life. I entertained despondency. I believed every lie Satan fed me, so much so that I became blinded to God's truth.

CHAPTER 06

The Life I Woke Up To
BY CHRIS

I'm caught in this tension: I desire to have a deep encounter with God, while at the same time too many circumstances and worldly priorities pull and tug so hard and so fast on me I feel 'buzzed' by it all. So, I just suck it up, get out of bed and carry on with trying to balance life's demands.

Coming first to my mind is that I have to get the girls up and off to school so Nancy can maximize her rest. I usually have no idea how her sleep went the night before. *Did she sleep through the night? Did she just fall asleep an hour ago?* No time to guess. I have to move quickly to my tasks. Get the girls up. Get myself ready. Make lunches. Empty the dishwasher. Feed the dog. Grab my backpack for work. Where are my keys? Get in the car!

Nancy and I worked it out in our marriage long ago that we each have areas of responsibility that we manage, but we share and delegate tasks under our management if we need help—

even to each other. More frequently I have been absorbing more of Nancy's responsibilities. Not all of them, but definitely more than I can handle.

Since her diagnosis in 2004, Nancy's area of responsibility includes the home front, meals, market runs, and taking care of the girls after school and until their bedtime (from 3:30 to 9:00). We continued this trend when we moved to Texas in 2006. She began transitioning out of full-time work as the Controller and CEO for our marketing agency in 2008.

I take care of getting the kids up and off to school, maintenance for our home and cars, and I help Nancy with anything she can't do. I also hang out with the kids after work, help with homework and school projects, and drive them where they need to be. I am heavily involved in anything athletic, sometimes as an assistant coach. I play indoor soccer on two adult teams with a bunch of fanatic 30-somethings. I enjoy a skate on my longboard. Every week I have a nagging worry about what orthopedic injuries I can avoid!

At the time of the writing of this chapter, I was also finishing a two-year post-graduate program in Biblical studies. I hardly watch any television.

But that still isn't the big gorilla in my life.

The largest pull for my time and attention is our business. I am a lifelong entrepreneur in the creative, branding and internet industry.

Long ago, I tried starting a newspaper. (That venture failed.) With Nancy, we started a freelance design business. (It petered out.) We marketed a dog collar product. (After a couple trade shows, we let that one stray. Ha!) Then, in 1995, I partnered with a friend in a design studio that took off. We eventually sold the company in 2000. That same year Nancy and I started a web hosting company. We even tried real estate investments that have done so-so.

Currently, Nancy and I own one main business called More Cabbage. Started in 2003 as a web design and branding firm, More Cabbage now manages social media as a public relations function for corporations. We have a team of about 19, including our employees and core freelancers.

For Nancy, who was trying to slow down the pace of life in order to deal with her health, a career in any service-based business related to internet marketing was the wrong industry to be in. The industry moves and changes far too fast to offer a slow pace. The client's needs are detailed, consuming and never-ending. Because of her intermittent attendance, Nancy was forced to make the gradual transition out of working for the company to dealing with health issues. However, this afforded her the time to rediscover her love for art, and she found joy in learning how to paint from the masters.

I like my business life and the challenges that come with it. After having gone through three major paradigm shifts in our industry, we are currently on the third "version" of the company, with our best team so far. We stay busy, and I travel about every two weeks for two or three days.

With the business comes maintaining balance between work life and home life. For example, when Nancy is suddenly out of energy, as her primary caregiver, I usually have to be ready and able to head home to help her or take over, however, it comes with the nagging feeling of knowing something is going unfinished at work.

While all this is going on, I begged God to please not let Satan touch the business. It was already showing signs of a down economy and I couldn't handle losing our business through all of this. I believe God clearly showed me through Scripture that He would protect and bless the business if we would just wait on Him.

We want to run our business for God. We believe it's from Him and we're thankful for it. We call it God's Sweet Gift to Us (drawing out the "e" in "sweet" like a surfer would say). I am very grateful to report that we've had many successful years where we've been able to serve clients', employees' and missionaries' needs.

December 2003 marks when God gave Nancy and me the idea to start More Cabbage, and a few months later, the very next spring, marks when Nancy was diagnosed with MS.

CHAPTER 07

P.O.W.

BY NANCY

It didn't occur to me until much later that my struggle with MS was not only physical, but spiritual, too, and the battle had to be fought on both fronts.

As much as our culture jokes about the "voices in our head," I know that everyone has different levels of confidence and self-talk. I believe the genesis of a confident thought does not come from my own mind but from the outside influence of others. It's planted there from those I have looked up to, probably at a young age and throughout my life. And since I *do* believe in God and Jesus, I know His words in my mind are good. I also believe there is a devil and one of his delights is to plant his lies in my head. He engages me in a battle to distract me away from God, from knowing His love and His plan for my life.

For example, to say I believe that God heals is one level of faith. To live with the effects of MS and still hold the conviction that

God heals is a whole other level. I would find myself questioning my own beliefs. This deeper level of spiritual battle left me feeling so ill-equipped, desperate and certain of defeat. I became convinced that I couldn't fight a spiritual battle when my body was physically weakened.

My prayers were, *"Where are You, Lord? What about the promises I've read about in Scripture about how you heal the sick? Why won't You heal me? Don't You care?"*

These were quiet prayers – the kind I wouldn't tell others I had been thinking about. I felt ashamed and embarrassed that I had a faith that crumbles at the sight of battle. I couldn't allow myself to express those raw thoughts, feelings and fears out loud. *No way! A mature Christian would say, "I will boast in my weakness for when I am weak then He is made strong."*

I tried with everything inside me to put up a brave front and suffer like a good little Christian soldier. In order to do this, I hid emotionally from others, which left me isolated and vulnerable to the enemy's schemes and lies. I was a sitting duck.

By isolating myself from others' prayers and healing words, I unconsciously built a self-constructed prison of pain. Then I gathered my belongings and moved right in. I resolved that this crippled identity was going to be my lot in life.

"Would you like to go out to lunch?" my friends would ask me.

"Sure, I'll join you." I sometimes didn't want to go, because I knew the conversation would eventually turn to me.

If I did go, and it became my turn to talk about what was *really* going on, I seemed to only see my life and my limitations in light of the disease. I could only talk about my defeats: my falls, my shortcomings, my lack of being able to do anything significant. The devil spoke clearly into my thoughts telling me that I was a difficult friend, or prickly or needy. On the other hand, my friends had no way of truly understanding that MS also affected my own thought process and cognition. I was already at a disadvantage before the conversation started.

My identity would become "MS." Nancy was *in* MS.

I reasoned that God's big plan for me was to allow me to have MS and somehow he would use it to bring Him honor and glory. I conceded that this sounded okay in theory, but the concept was not sitting well with me at all. I often wrestled with this truth: God heals. *So, Lord, why won't You heal me completely? Wouldn't that really bring You glory?*

I recalled this Bible verse: **For our struggle is not against flesh and blood, but against the rulers, against the authorities, against the powers of this dark world and against the**

spiritual forces of evil in the heavenly realms.

Ephesians 6:12 New International Version (NIV)

I recall it was early on in my faith, when I chose to follow Jesus, I knew I would become a partaker in God's Kingdom. However, at that time, I was also naive to the fact and that an opposite, dark kingdom would also press in on me and try to overtake me. Make no mistake. There is an enemy and his name is Satan. In essence, when I became a true Christian, I entered into a war.

Coming to the realization that spiritual warfare is a reality is somewhat like signing up for the military to get a great education, see the world and receive all these wonderful benefits – only to discover that as soon as I step onto the battlefield, I am expected to shoot a gun, deal with wartime strategies, take marching orders and withstand enemy fire! *How* I respond to the fact that I'm in a spiritual war *affects* my outcome whether I'm victorious or defeated. Will I fight or flee? Will I let the enemy overtake me with fear, or will I stand firm, disciplined and courageous for His Kingdom?

How do I prevent the enemy from defeating me, from gaining access to my thought life? How do I avoid becoming a prisoner of war? How am I supposed to fight a spiritual battle I can't see?

Every follower of Christ experiences this reality at some point in our walk with God: Whether or not I choose to believe it to be true, *I am* most definitely engaged in a spiritual war. The side I wanted to be on offered love and life. The other side wanted to take my life from me. I was already in a weakened state, so defeat became a very real threat.

My questions continued. *How much influence does the enemy have in my daily life? Is it only my thought-life he attacks? Was he somehow behind the argument Chris and I had today? Did he cause the dishwasher and the dryer to break on the same day? Did he give me MS? Was that Satan?!*

I noticed that the enemy launched his attacks by getting in his little digs wherever he could. *Isn't the battle Yours to fight, Lord? Where are You?* He tried to convince me that I was alone and use-less, that God was nowhere to be found, that He abandoned me. This thinking would only lead me deeper into hopelessness.

Throughout my life when I wasn't close with God compared to times when I was, I've come to know different forms of attack, for example, like an addiction that crept up on me whenever I let my guard down. Although addictions can take many forms, in my case, drinking and drugs were my attempt to escape from that emotional pain I was in. I developed these destructive be-haviors from a very early age.

I've learned from personal experience that it's difficult to carry on an addiction and trust God at the same time. These cannot co-exist. They are like great white sharks and seals. Seals cannot swim with sharks. The outcome is obvious; the shark will devour the seal. And so it is with addiction. It is impossible to practice addiction and practice the "presence of God." You can surely commit to one or the other – it just can't be both.

If my desire to serve God is divided by looking to other de-sires, like drinking or medicating or checking out, how would I stand? How would God's presence prevail in my life, having a divided heart?

There have been many seasons of my adult life when I have cho-sen to practice the presence of God – a life of trusting God and turning to Him in all things, a life surrendered to God.

In other seasons, I scarcely stood strong. I lacked courage and discipline. I simply had a hard time trusting that God was going to make me victorious. I had chosen to fall into temptation, de-scending into old patterns of depression, anger and self-pity, and falling victim to the destruction of the enemy.

And so in this season I succumbed to the attack the enemy was making on my life through MS by allowing it to become my identity and giving in to depression and despondency. It was as if a suffocating, spiritual blanket had been tossed over me and dark forces carried me away. I floundered and beat the air until I was rendered completely exhausted. My attempt to set myself free

P.O.W.

from the snare of the enemy was futile. I had been captured.

I became a prisoner of war.

CHAPTER 08

Sick of Being Sick
BY CHRIS

It was the summer of 2008 when we took a cruise to the Western Caribbean. We figured that a cruise was the right kind of vacation our family could take providing both restful opportunities and activities that we could all participate in.

What we didn't factor in was the two-hour wait required to board the ship. Nancy had to stand the entire time in a hot, humid line and haul a piece luggage. I already had three suitcases in tow, and the girls had small bags they were holding.

Exacerbated by the heat and the physical exhaustion, Nancy's MS flared up. It caused her nerves to short-circuit.

Nancy transitioned from having highly functional days prior to the cruise to non-functional days on-board, with an empty fuel tank and a despondent reaction to her predicament.

Nightly, Nancy would collapse into bed exhausted at 8:00 pm, after having already napped once and sometimes twice earlier in the day. She had no wheelchair or cane to support her walking on the big ship.

She never fully recovered from that trip, and her condition deteriorated. Because her exacerbation was subtle, I couldn't see its effect on a day-to-day basis. Without the intervention of a steroid infusion or treatment regimen, the condition manifesting during a flare-up gradually worsened, which is what happened to Nancy on the cruise.

About a month after the cruise was over, I really noticed it.

We returned from an exhausting vacation with the prolonged effects of MS having overwhelmed Nancy. The best way I can describe it is her physical and mental condition shifted from 80% before the trip to about 35% after.

I prayed for her again, but I lacked motivation and felt repetitive with God. I think I also started to resign to the idea that this was how life was going to be. I was settling. I'm sure I had some frustration and grief mixed in there, too.

I need to confess that after a few years I got tired of praying for healing – not because I stopped loving Nancy or my faith was gone. It's more like my trust or belief wasn't stirred up 24 hours a day, seven days a week. I would lose focus. Sometimes I resolved that God already heard me, so my praying amounted to pounding repetitively on His door, annoying Him. Again and again. *It's been years, doesn't He already know what I'm going to ask before I ask it?*

And yet, I know God can heal, and I didn't believe He was denying Nancy His power just because He hadn't healed her *yet*. I love and trust God no matter *when* He heals her. Whether now or later or when she dies – she will be free. I know it.

I tried to cope by separating myself from what she was going through. If she was going to end up in bed at 8:00, then I figured I might as well just start working nights. I got into the routine of leaving work at 4:00 p.m. to help out more in the late afternoon with the kids and then working from home in the evenings after Nancy went to bed.

In November of the same year (2008), three months after the cruise, we got more bad news; an ultrasound detected a large tumor on Nancy's uterus. By mid-December, a surgery was necessary to remove the tumor and uterus. The tumor was benign, thank God. However, an MRI also revealed many new MS lesions (or scars) on her brain and spinal cord. The disease was rapidly progressing.

The surgery in December left Nancy with two "gems." First,

45

the anesthesiologist opened Nancy's jaw too wide when he was intubating her, causing her jaw to be dislocated and leaving her in intense jaw pain for several months. Second, the stress of the surgery and loss of her uterus threw Nancy into *another* MS exacerbation. This time, the disease seemed to mostly affect her balance. She was falling – a lot. A cane, then, a wheelchair became necessary wherever she went.

Nancy and I knew, but didn't want to admit, that she was physically and emotionally falling apart. She was sick of being sick.

We were struggling through the feelings of anger and apathy, surrendering to the notion that this was our lot in life. We didn't have a healthy perspective on what our lot was. In fact, we lived in this absent place somewhere between disease management and wanting a healing from God without knowing how to fully commit to either. It left us a bit aimless.

Now, while it seems logical that there are services and help for people in our situation, we just hadn't arrived at this conclusion yet. We had been in a state of slow acceptance of the disease as the MS got worse. We were not spiritually healthy nor as close to God as we should have been at this point in time.

Nancy told me. "I'm not doing well and we need some support."

"I know." I replied. "I wanted to talk to you about getting some help and how I feel about it. I've been praying and asking God for a healing. But I'm tired of asking too. There are so many scenarios that are closing in on us—I'm not spending enough time with you, we're running low on cash, we're not experiencing a healing breakthrough, I don't know where to turn next. So I've been meaning to talk to you," I continued, "I'm not sure where I stand about getting some help with disability benefits. I mean, I feel like we're basically resolving that we don't believe God is going to heal, so we need to take some other sort of action. You're already struggling with being present at work."

"And we need help with the medical expenses." Nancy noted. "It's up to $1700 a month right now, since the surgery."

"And it means handicapped placards and taking a handout from the government," I said aloud.

"And getting a disabled label on me," Nancy added.

"And there are lots of mental pictures I get with that," I retorted.

As we kept following this line of thinking, Nancy and I felt that managing the disease medically and applying for disability benefits resigned us both to the idea that this was a permanent, debilitating disease. We imagined MS would eventually prevent her from painting and walking and might possibly end with her slumped over in a wheelchair. It would mean doctor's visits, extra time required wherever we go, and life experiences we could no longer participate in. Perhaps most disappointing of all, I would have to resolve that we would NOT be examples of God's healing. Rather, we would be a pathetic visual aid represented to the world that either God didn't care or He was impotent. My attitude was so judgmental; it mixed right into our raw thoughts.

So for some time, we didn't want a wheelchair. We had not filed for any disability benefits or handicapped placards. We were afraid of the outcome, the label, and the mental picture it created in our minds.

Was our faith weak?

We wanted our lives to be different. If only we could exercise together again. Or work outside together in the backyard. Or chase each other around the house. We were grieving our yesterdays, stuck there because we couldn't let go.

Too many times I felt like a single parent while Nancy seemed forced to stay home and close to bed so she could rest. Often I would show up at a function at church, a gymnastics practice or a kid's open house at school with just Rebekah and Meghan – the three of us. We were creating memories together, without Nancy.

Nancy also suffered from depression believing her value as a woman, a wife and a mother had diminished. She often commented about feeling useless, about being a burden to us. She lamented the reality that her body was giving out. She voiced her fears about not being able to paint in the future. All of these took up residence in her mind. She contemplated the "easy" path of getting out of this world and wanting to go be with Jesus. I didn't recognize how toxic this kind of thinking was. We both had previously spoken casually about being with Jesus—it's definitely a good plan, and we desire it—but only when God is ready to make that happen. I gave her space for her thoughts because I believed it was her way of processing all this.

Nancy, however, started to rationalize that being in heaven had become her *only* option rather than living here on earth. On several occasions, usually on down days, she told me that she would be free if she could just be in the presence of the Lord. I truly didn't know what to say or how to react. I just knew she was in pain and she wanted out.

"I'm going to head to bed," Nancy said.

"It's only 7:30. Did you nap today?" I just finished eating dinner and looked at the pile of dishes.

"Yes, of course I napped." Nancy's voice was defensive, and yet, suppressed because of her weakness. "And I'm sick of my energy levels being so low I can't stand up any longer."

"Why don't you go and lie down and watch a movie or something and I'll get the kitchen," I offered, reluctantly, because I really had other things to do.

I enabled her with lots of free time to rest; but with the best of intentions to create a healing environment, I just accepted a larger burden on my shoulders, and the burden was getting heavier.

Nancy also told me – frequently – that she was a burden to *me*, and that the family would be better off without her. Though I tried to assure her otherwise, I think the fact that I was always "on," as a parent, husband, homeowner, church leader and business leader, made me look as if I was running at a fast pace – a pace that Nancy was done trying to keep up with. If Nancy was comparing, I was the wrong person to measure against. By my activity, I was projecting that the speed of life is ultra fast, and if you can't keep up, you can't participate. I had little perspective on Nancy's needs. Reality was that *I* was barely holding it together.

However, I had a saving grace. I had a team—a strong, personal support network among staff and friends. Whenever a surgery happened or Nancy was in the hospital, we had some very kind neighbors and friends from church who were available to us, and they would step in to supply us with meals or pick up and watch our kids. I felt like I could call on many friends to help me out, and I did. In this season, I thanked God for Joani Dockery and Linda Agnew who helped free me up at work so I could handle the demands on our household. There is no way I could have functioned without my support network.

By this time, however, Nancy had more or less isolated herself from her support. She was depressed. She looked despondent and said she felt defeated. If Satan wanted to incinerate her, all he would have to do was light a match because the lighter fluid was already poured.

It was a dark season, and I longed for a respite. Unfortunately, the times that I wanted to rest didn't coincide with the demands on our life during these months.

Sometimes a couple days of business travel gave me a few hours where no demands were placed on me. Normally, after a long day, I usually found my rest between 11:00 pm and midnight in a cold 12-ounce bottle of Corona and an episode on Netflix, while engaging in Facebook. I know there are better ways to rest, but I chose this form of escape. My spiritual condition did not improve because I wasn't making enough deposits by reading the Word of God. I knew I needed the words in the Bible to strengthen me, but I found too many excuses to ignore them.

Interestingly enough, I did continue to pray that the Lord would draw me out of whatever funk we were in. I prayed that Nancy and I would both be delivered into a better life with Christ. I wanted the big miracle.

It was late March 2009, the same month I had the "emergency landing" dream. It was several months after Nancy's surgery, and we consulted with our neurologist again.

Nancy was in a prolonged exacerbated state. The neurologist said the stress of the hysterectomy was too much for her and she needed another steroid infusion. We scheduled it immediately. During the first week of April, she was at home hooked up to an IV bag. This was followed by a course of oral steroids, another medication that Nancy did not tolerate well. The effects of the steroids would intensify all the negative feelings she was experiencing. It came with the side effects of depression and caused weight gain—another struggle Nancy had been lamenting over.

During that time, we were hosting houseguests who didn't fully grasp the gravity of our situation. We, of course, were attempting to put on a happy face. In hindsight, a saner approach would have been to cancel on the houseguests rather than adding to the stress.

It was a sad time. I grabbed my longboard and went for a skate. I needed to be by myself. I headed down the street and started thinking about how much care I would need to give Nancy. I started thinking about the future plans I would be giving up on. I would challenge myself, *"How can I free up even more time to be at home?"* I considered selling the business because I determined I couldn't keep running it and be with Nancy. Maybe we can get by without working by moving in with someone or getting a mobile home. I was conflicted because Nancy and I always spoke of More Cabbage as God's Sweet Gift to Us. *Do I have to give the gift back?*

It was the first time I experienced a panic attack. I had to stop riding and sit down on the curb. I took several deep breaths. It finally passed after I re-centered on the reality that God is in control, not me.

I remember telling a few close friends, "My life is crashing."

CHAPTER 09

Our Friends Interpret the Dream
BY CHRIS

It had been about three weeks since I had the "emergency landing" dream and it was nagging me. I emailed my dream to Paul Jones and Heather Harbaugh and asked if they had a sense of how to interpret it and its symbolism. I figured that since they were both in the dream and had a gift for interpreting dreams, God would show them what it meant.

Heather prayerfully took on my request and asked God about the dream. She also asked Paul to join us for a time of prayer and communion the following week on Tuesday, April 7, 2009.

Heather showed up with a bag of items. As she began to share her thoughts, Nancy and I were touched that she had taken the time to seriously consider the dream, pray about it and respond to us.

Paul showed up with a loaf of French bread and grape juice.

Heather started. "I believe the plane is your ministry to each other and to the church. It is crashing.

I believe the Aztec structure reflects something ancient in your lives, something that you have been reflecting in your walk with the Lord."

I wondered what this meant. *Had we built up an ancient structure of self-reliance?* Certainly we were not getting anywhere on our own strength.

Heather continued, "I think the multicolored tools I offered in the dream have significance in addressing the plane crash and the structure, and I wanted to spend the time to ask the Lord what the tools were that He would have me give you."

"The first is a CD of affirmations. They are read by evangelist and author, Patricia King, and are directly out of the Word to affirm the promises of God. We often forget these promises so this will be an encouragement to you and will have life-giving power. Listen to them. Speak them out over yourself and each other. Repeat them."

I had always believed that affirming oneself with words is powerful. However, in our marriage, I seemed to conveniently forget that God's Words uttered aloud have the most power to affect the outcome. I welcomed the idea of using God's Words and

Promises instead of my own words.

"The second is a phone number," Heather added. " I just felt led to give you a phone number for a Spirit-filled counselor from Gateway Grand Prairie, who I think might have some answers." I assumed this was for Nancy.

"The third is a hundred dollars. And I'm not sure why I'm supposed to give you this." I reluctantly accepted it.

At this point, I thought of a single mother in the church, Crista Darr, who, out of the blue, gave us $100 just three days earlier. "Very unusual," I thought. I had asked Crista what the Lord was showing her. In other words, why would she do this? She shrugged it off, saying, "I don't know. God will show you." Her gift was hard to receive. She was a single mom with greater needs than mine, I arrogantly thought, whom I wanted to support, not the other way around.

Did this mean God was telling us that He would be providing for our financial needs on a new level? Our needs have always been met, but did this action symbolize more to come? It was a little difficult to receive the money from Heather as well because I knew that her husband was out of work at that time and her family had financial needs of their own. This was just another demonstration of her strength of faith and her obedience to do what she believed God was telling her to do. I also had a lesson in learning to receive.

Heather continued. "The last tool is a silk shawl. I hand-painted this scene on it, showing the communion elements and the words from Luke 22:19-20."

"…And he took bread, gave thanks and broke it, and gave it to them, saying, 'This is my body given for you; do this in remembrance of me.' In the same way, after the supper he took the cup, saying, 'This cup is the new covenant in my blood, which is poured out for you.'"

As I looked closely at the shawl, I noticed in small words repeated all around the border: It is finished. Death is beaten.

Heather thought the Lord was saying to wrap the silk around Nancy while we took communion. Every day. From here forward. I was to serve Nancy.

We started right then. I did my very best to use the shawl. It was hard to have a ceremony every day, and I wasn't successful. However, if one thing stuck with me, it was the affirmations. From that moment, I was convinced that speaking the Word of God, out loud, over others and myself, was like wielding a superpower. Ever since then, battles have been fought—and won. Really cool outcomes, or blessings, have come into play in our life simply from speaking out God's life-giving words in the Bible.

While Heather and Paul prayed for us, I saw a picture in my

mind where I was driving a vehicle on a long trip with Nancy as a passenger. The steering wheel kept tugging me to the side. I said, "I think the Lord is showing me that we are out of alignment. Nancy and I are headed in the same direction, in the same car even, but we are not aligned." I over-interpreted it at this point when I said, "I also think that just like I'm not aligned to the Father, Nancy is not aligned to me." I probably should have kept that one to myself and prayed about it later.

After saying that, Heather and Paul grew quiet; it was an awkward moment. She broke the tension when Heather said, "Chris, I believe the counselor's phone number is for you!"

I did have to agree. My life *and* my mind were out of alignment from months of build-up. I needed help to work through and process what was going on. As the caregiver in this situation, I also had needs. I couldn't keep sweeping my losses, needs and pain under a rug without leaving a large mound. My problem though, was that I didn't seem to ever take the time to realize how long I had been sweeping.

CHAPTER 10

Not a Very Good Friday
BY CHRIS

The day after Paul and Heather came over to interpret the dream and pray with us, I boarded a plane for Los Angeles from Dallas. (We currently live in Dallas, Texas, which is a story for another time.)

Since our business originated in California, I often have clients and work to do there. After two days, I was back in Texas on Thursday, late in the evening. Nancy was already in bed. She had spent two full days with the girls, now nine and eleven. This meant despite how she felt or whatever was going on, she still had the responsibility of getting them to school and back home, to rock climbing and gymnastics, and, hopefully, fed, homework done and in bed without incident.

I don't know all that happened during these two days, but by Friday morning, I can tell you that Nancy was completely depleted. There was no life left in her. I would describe it as the overwhelming combination of not being able to walk, her jaw aching, feeling numb from MS, feeling like God wasn't answering any more prayers – and I'm sure the girls and I contributed to her empty state by placing demands on her over the previous two days.

We had planned to go to the Good Friday service at our church that evening, but we were totally out of gas. Days like this always translated into "Let's all 'check out' as a family and watch a movie." So that's what we did. It was such a miserably inadequate existence. Not a very "Good Friday," I thought. I noticed Nancy sinking deeper into depression, more than usual.

We had arranged to take spring family photos the very next day, Saturday. Nancy looked pretty, but she was heavily medicated. To borrow a phrase from Alcoholics Anonymous, I could tell she was "trying to bring her body so that her mind would follow." Some of the images from this family photo shoot captured her condition. You could see it in her eyes. She looked incredibly distant, drugged, defeated. She was just going through the motions but not really present.

The Lord had put in my mind a couple weeks before to tell Nancy, everyday, that she is beautiful. I didn't yet realize it was training me to affirm our love with the Word of God. After all, it was my superpower. Speaking this over her reminded me who and why I married, and helped prepare me for the spiritual battle of my life.

CHAPTER 11

I Just Want to Be with Jesus

BY NANCY

I'm so tired. Every day. All the time. I feel weak. I feel depressed. I can't contribute. I'm a burden to my family. My head hurts. My jaw hurts. My eyes are heavy. I'm on eleven medications and I have to take another four to counteract the eleven I'm on. I can't feel parts of my body. I can't feel my right leg so I drop my foot when I walk, if I can walk. My back now aches because I walk funny. I can't pee without a catheter because I'm numb from the waist down. I live with a chronic bladder infection. I think I'm constipated, but I don't know, I can't feel anything. There's no more pleasure in love-making. An orgasm is out of the question. I just want to be with you Jesus.

CHAPTER 12

Resurrection Sunday
BY CHRIS

The next day was Easter morning, Resurrection Sunday, and Nancy and I were getting ready for church.

We had all done a fast for Lent – a time to give up something for the 40 days that led up to Easter so we could identify with the sufferings and resurrection of Christ.

My "suffering" was pretty weak—the attempt was half-hearted at best. I gave up checking emails first thing in the morning and, instead, waited until after I took the girls to school. I was supposed to use that time to pray, but I used it to sleep. Bekah had given up dessert. Meghan, being clever, thought that she could give up school for Lent, but after explaining the purpose of Lent, she reconsidered. Meghan ultimately decided on no gum (this actually *was* a sacrifice for her). Nancy had taken a break from coffee.

7:30 AM, Sunday, April 12, 2009

I had awoken, made Nancy a cup of coffee for break fast (get it?), and caught Bekah eating a sugar doughnut for her break fast. I took the cup of coffee into our bathroom and started talking with Nancy.

Within moments we started arguing about how I hadn't included Nancy in a conversation I'd had with Bekah about the cell phone she was working toward earning. I had made some decisions about how we would go about it and started informing Bekah before I had spoken with Nancy. Since lately I had felt more empowered by managing the house affairs, having taken over for Nancy, and picking up on her despondent cues, I had assumed it was okay to call the shots. Nancy had every right to be angry with me for presenting my decision to Bekah as if it were ours – even though we had not even discussed it.

Already in a tense moment, things suddenly got disproportionately out of control. "And another thing," Nancy argued emphatically, "I don't like that you brought up the alignment issue!"

I was taken aback because those words never came out of my mouth that morning. *"What voice just spoke to her?"* I wondered. *"Where did that come from? Was she referring to last Tuesday with Heather and Paul?"*

I argued back, "I never said that, so don't tell me I did."

The argument went from hot to boiling. In the course of about two minutes, I decided that I did not want to spend Easter with Nancy because she was blowing things out of proportion and I couldn't handle the volatility of her emotional state. I thought it would be best that she and I just do our own, separate thing that morning.

"I don't want to be with you this morning," I said to hurt her. "You take the kids and go to church."

"No!" she yelled. "YOU take the kids and go to church. I'm staying here!"

"Fine!"

"Fine!"

I finished getting ready, sulking the whole time. I grabbed the keys and summoned Bekah and Meghan into the car so the three of us – again – would be together. This time, however, it was a holiday that all four of us should have celebrated together.

10:00 AM

It's really hard to be at church after an argument. I can't hide my hurt very well. About 20 people came up to me to ask how I was doing. They were all smiles, with nice Easter outfits.

"Well," I wanted to begin, "Nancy and I had a major blow-out. I was in her face and hurt her. Work is on my mind, and I'm worried about our company's survival. I have no peace. Nancy is on a bunch of steroids and behaving in difficult and despondent ways… Our marriage is a wreck…"

While we belonged to a mature church, with lots of transparency, I just had a hard time bringing up conversations like that on Easter, so I didn't. *It's a celebration day! He is Risen, and all that goodness, right?!* Besides, I felt like I would be betraying Nancy's confidence by bringing up something so personal without her present to defend herself. So I didn't.

Instead, I shared light stuff; in the language of Christianese, like, "we're struggling a bit right now so pray for God's grace on us." I felt odd saying anything more than that. It was sad too, because in the battle we were fighting, we really needed some heavy artillery in the form of prayer. I felt wimpy around the church that day. I must have looked like the poster child for lonely.

Just before we left, a friend of ours, Linda Agnew, approached me and asked if Nancy might like to join her and Heather in Redding, California for a healing conference. I said, "Just what she needs! And Nancy really likes Bill Johnson and the worship coming from Bethel. Thank you for thinking of her!"

12:15 PM

Church is out, and I swept the kids into the car because we had
to go to the market to pick up a couple of things. My parents,
my sister and her husband with our toddling nephew, Luke,
were coming over later for Easter dinner.

I had coordinated Easter dinner with them because Nancy wasn't
feeling well, and I wanted to have Easter at our house. In times
past, I would be the one to initiate a social gathering, but then I'd
leave it to Nancy to pull it together mostly on her own. At this
point in our lives, if I wanted to have a gathering, it was up to me
to plan it and make it happen – especially my favorite holiday.

So I delegated the ham responsibility to my mom, the potatoes
to my sis, and I took care of the rest. But I was out of olives for
the salad, and I needed to see if there were any plastic eggs at
Super Target. I wanted to fill them with Cheerios and hide them
all over the front lawn for Luke.

1:00 PM

Super Target was out of everything "Easter," so the girls and I
bought just the olives and headed home.

When we arrived home, our bedroom door was closed, and I
didn't want to disturb Nancy's sleeping.

69

I tried to keep the girls quiet while I prepared in the kitchen.

At some point I had to make a trip to the bedroom, and I opened the door softly, but Nancy wasn't there.

"Oh," I thought.

I checked our garage and, sure enough, our SUV, Big Red, was gone.

I tried phoning Nancy on her cell. I got her voicemail, so I left a message. "Hi, Nancy, it's me. I was just wondering where you're at. Gimme a call."

A long time ago, we got this list of guidelines from a counselor called "Fair Fighting Rules." It has helped us in our relationship tremendously. It is a simple sheet with communication statements to use while in an argument. Some of the "Rules" are just plain wise.

I remember a few: 1) Always use "I" statements to express your feelings. 2) Never drag your relatives into your side of the argument (because it makes the spouse appear evil to the in-laws, and then it's out there and you can't take it back). 3) During a heated argument, things are usually said out of anger and are not true indications of where the person is. 4) Anger implies hurt, so give the person time to get their hurt communicated. 5) Listen and reflect what you heard. 6) If you need some time away from the other person, just say you need some space. If you leave home, write a note if need be, and mention when you'll be back to talk again.

To this day, we try to practice Fair Fighting Rules. I suppose it lets us love with healthy boundaries. It also lets us cool down before we say something hurtful or stupid.

That Sunday afternoon, I went to the kitchen to look for the note. The note from the Fair Fighting Rules that would say, "I ended up going to a different church today for service. Be back soon. We'll talk after dinner."

I couldn't find a note.

3:00 PM

I tried calling Nancy again. Her phone rang twice and I got voicemail. "Hey, Nancy, it's me. I wanted to know where you're at because my parents will be here in about 30 minutes. Talk to you later."

I figured she needed some space. It was not unusual for Nancy. A number of times throughout our relationship, when she and I argued intensely, Nancy would be the one to head out and cool down. Usually, she would end up at a friend's house, spend a few hours there, talk it out, get some prayer – and then she'd come home, and we'd talk about our mistakes and forgive each other.

This time, I started getting angry because I thought she was bailing on Easter just to get me aggravated. She was chillin' at a friend's house, enjoying the dinner and company, and I was at home preparing parts of our Easter dinner by myself. And she didn't leave me a note!

3:28 PM

The doorbell rang. It was my parents. Prompt as usual. When they didn't see Nancy coming to greet them, they asked where she was. "She's out right now," I reported. "She needed some space today, and she couldn't do Easter, so we decided she needed to take care of herself." I made it sound like we were both in this decision together. I was covering for Nancy. Then I let it go, and refocused on my family to enjoy my favorite holiday.

We pressed on with Easter dinner. It was really fun. It was a bummer not having Nancy with us because we had a nice time. It was a joy with Luke there and catching up on the latest stories.

5:27 PM

During the gathering, I tried calling Nancy again because my girls had been asking where Mom was. When I called her phone this time, it immediately went to voicemail. It does this when the phone is switched off. I didn't leave a message because I had already left two.

Immediately I assumed she went to see a movie by herself, something she's done before, but I was feeling angry that she didn't respect me enough to tell me. I told the girls that I thought Mom was at a movie (I hoped she was) and that she would be home later (I hoped she would).

7:05 PM

Shortly before my family left, they helped me do the dishes. I appreciated this. It gave me time to hang out with my girls some more. I went outside to watch them bounce on the trampoline, then I got on the trampoline and bounced with them. We finally laid down on the trampoline, stared up into the beautiful sky and shared some Easter candy. We said silly things and laughed.

Not long after, I phoned Nancy again, but this time I left a voicemail. "Hey," I said, "I'm starting to get a little worried, and I'd like to know where you are. My parents are gone now, so if you're wanting to return home, it's just us."

9:50 PM

I put the girls to bed and read some from the Bible to them. At bedtime, we had been reading about the events leading up to Jesus' resurrection all week, so this was *the* big moment: when He rose from the dead.

After the girls were down, I called Nancy again. Straight to voicemail. This time I was concerned, so I had a little angry threat in my tone. "Nancy, if you went to see a movie, it would be done by now. You need to call me right away. If you do not, I *will* call the police and report you as missing."

11:30 PM

Still no call. So I did it. I called the police station to report that my wife was missing. They said they would need to send an officer to the house. I inquired if they "could do it discreetly, because my kids are asleep" (and I was embarrassed to have a cop car outside my house). They started fishing on the phone for some information that I was reluctant to give out. In part, I was in denial, part of it was embarrassment, part of it was fear.

Nevertheless, I complied and subjected myself to the probing quiz, which earned me an officer's visit and a patrol car in front of my house.

CHAPTER 13

Crash and Burn
BY NANCY

It was Easter Sunday and, while getting ready for church, we started fighting. Chris and I had a huge crash-and-burn blowout. I was seething mad and screamed at the top of my lungs, "Take the girls and go to church – just *get out of here!*" Well, I didn't have to say that twice. Chris and the girls took off, and I, from that moment on, went on automatic pilot. I set out on a mission.

Now, of course, the plan I was about to execute was not a new idea, nor was it out of the blue. It's one that had been marinating in my mind for a long time, an outcome I had alluded to many times over to many people, including Chris.

I finished getting dressed, and, as I did, I remember feeling a strange sort of calm settling over me. All the lies and recordings that had been ruminating in my mind for months were about to become a reality, and I was greatly relieved. I didn't realize it at the time, but the recordings in my thoughts were from the enemy, repetitive in nature, all negative and lacking in truth. For example, I would literally hear, "You are worthless; everyone would be better off if you were dead; you'll be doing everyone a favor."

I had convinced myself that I would do the *right* thing by relieving my family from the burden of *me*.

In my mind my new name had become Burden. Unfortunately, I had stopped asking God what He thought about me. Instead, I decided to listen to and agree with the enemy of my soul about *his* opinion of me. I call this "making agreements with the enemy." It's when I give credence to the lies of Satan and come to accept the lies in my head as truth. So with that, I reasoned:

Chris is a great guy. He'll have no problem finding an awesome wife, one who is attentive – not a burden – one who can be the helpmate and mother that I can't be.

My condition is a burden to others. I am ashamed of who I am and who I have become.

I hate that I can't contribute, that I always need others to help me with the basic functions in life.

I just want to be with You, Jesus. I can't do this – I can't do life. It's become way too hard.

CRASH AND BURN

You're not healing me Lord, and this horrible disease isn't going to get better. It's only going to go downhill from here.

With an eerie, methodical progression, I rounded up my Bible, journal, and all the medications from my medicine cabinet that I thought would do the job. I felt relief that I was finally going to make all this pain and suffering go away. I felt a sense of calm at the idea that soon I would be with Jesus.

I looked at my beloved dog, Emmah, and whispered, "Good-bye." I stroked her face as her huge brown eyes pierced my soul as if they were saying, "Please don't leave me," but I couldn't even "hear" her.

I turned and walked out the door and drove off in Big Red.

My first stop was the CVS pharmacy where I refilled all of my 90-day prescriptions: Xanax, Vicodin, and Ambien, three of the more powerful anti-anxiety, pain-killing and sleeping pills a physician can prescribe. Any of these medications combined or taken alone in quantities exceeding the prescribed amount can be potentially fatal, and I knew it. I was counting on it.

As I walked toward the back of the store to the pharmacy counter, I noticed a woman walking toward me. Our eyes met and she smiled at me. Needless to say, I was in no mood to smile. My countenance must have said it all, "About-to-be-dead-woman-walking." Here's the weird part: as we passed each other, her friendly smile turned to a knowing smirk, her eyes narrowed at me and she said in a snide, devious tone, "Good-bye…"

Man! If I'd had any batteries left in my flashlight, I would have recognized the enemy right then and there! It was the personification of Satan, tipping his cards! He was showing me that he had won the game the moment I believed and acted on all those lies he fed me. But, alas, my batteries had already been drained. I was completely in the dark.

While at the pharmacy, I bought three greeting cards: one for Chris, one for Rebekah and one for Meghan. Next, I grabbed some Visine. I had recently watched one of those CSI TV shows and someone killed the victim by poisoning her with Visine. *It can't hurt – well, actually, it can. That's the point –never mind!* I added it to my cart.

Two more stops and I could get on with the business of making all this sorrow and suffering go away and enter into the presence of my Lord and my King. *I sure hope He's happy to see me!*

I stopped at Wal-Mart and got a coffee bean grinder and a little blender. (I'd heard that grinding the pills was the most efficient way to consume a large quantity of drugs for maximum results.)

I drove through Sonic and purchased my favorite drink, a

Lemon-Berry Cream Slush. I was actually getting excited to sprint down streets of gold to the Pearly Gates. Off I headed for a hotel.

Now finding a hotel was a bit of a lengthy process. I was thinking a room with a view of a lake might be nice, or maybe something overlooking a greenbelt. *What was I thinking?! Who cares?!* I drove all over for quite a while until I landed at the Hampton Inn.

The lady at the desk was so kind. She even helped me get my bag of stuff to the room. I paid cash for the room. I didn't want Chris to track me down by checking our credit card transactions. I felt pretty bad that I was going to lay this nightmare trip on this nice lady. I got over it – after all, I *was* on a mission and nothing was going to deter me.

The room was quiet because the walls were thick with insulation. The linens on the bed looked comfortable and clean. The room was light and bright, too cheery for my taste. I pulled the curtains shut thinking, *I never did find that lake view.* I went to work penning my thoughts before I prepared the last cocktail I would ever drink.

As I sat down at the desk and began to write in the cards, I tried to connect thought to paper while I poured out my heart to my daughters. *What does a mother say at a time like this? What does she leave them with under such circumstances?* As I write this account now, I can't believe I thought I could ever say anything that would make any sense of this. My reasoning was just so far out there! How deceived I had become!

Next was my farewell to Chris. It was my feeble and pathetic attempt to convince him that I was doing all of this for his own good and that, because I was burdening him, we'd all be better off in the end. I sealed the letters in with the cards and put everything neatly on the desk. I also included my emergency contact information for the police or paramedics to find so they could notify Chris of my death.

This was it.

It was 5:00 pm when I took the lid off of all the pill bottles and grinded the contents into a powdered form. I poured just a portion of the Sonic drink, the powdery substance and the bottle of Visine into the single-serving blender and spun it for a minute. The liquid was no longer icy and had melted enough so it would be easy to drink.

I raised the blend to my lips and began to down my concoction. It was cold and chalky, but it went down quickly. In just a matter of seconds, I was glad to be done with it.

I set the blender on the counter and I looked at the bed. I figured I had a minute before my brain would be on fire from the chemistry, then my heart would decrescendo to a very slow beat, where finally it would eventually stop, and I would breathe my last.

Within seconds I crawled into bed and surrounded myself with pillows. I curled up in the fetal position, holding one of the pillows close to me and started to feel the effects of the medication.

As I closed my eyes, I whispered to the Lord, *"Please receive me into Your Kingdom. I just want to be with You today. I love You, my Lord…"*

That's the last thing I remember.

But each one is tempted when he is drawn away by his own desires and enticed. Then, when desire has conceived, it gives birth to sin; and sin, when it is full-grown, brings forth death. Do not be deceived, my beloved brethren.

James 1:14-16 New American Standard Bible (NASB)

CHAPTER 14

An Early Monday Meeting
BY CHRIS

1:15 AM, Monday, April 13, 2009

I was upstairs, staring out the window. I was so afraid at the core that I forgot to pray. Praying is usually the first place I run when I'm upset… but I was paralyzed with fear. It was a fear-based reality that caused me to not know what to do. My breathing was short. It felt very dark and creepy, like a thick cloud moving over me. Even now as I write this, the feeling returns to me of shuddering, wondering where Nancy was. *Was she hurt? Did she drive into the lake? Was she even alive?*

I saw the officer pull up. I hurried downstairs to intercept him before he knocked on the door. I ushered him quickly into our study and closed the door. I sat while he stood. He took down a lot of information, including our social security numbers.

An hour earlier I had logged into our credit card account online.

It said that a charge went through for $68.72 at a local pharmacy at about 12:20 pm on Easter. I thought that maybe Nancy had picked up a couple prescriptions. There was also a debit charge for $170.00 at Wal-Mart at about 1:30 pm. The Wal-Mart purchase I couldn't guess at, except that the amount was even, so whatever she bought, she probably took some cash too.

The officer asked me, "What happened today?"

"Well," I said, "Nancy and I got in an argument this morning before church. When I returned home with my girls, she was gone. That's not too out of the ordinary for us." I continued, "But what's strange is that there was no note. She usually leaves a note or lets me know she needs to cool off somewhere. If I were to call her and leave a message, she'll call back and let me know she needs more time. I left messages for her all day. She missed Easter dinner. Her phone was on earlier today, but now her phone is completely off. I know she went to the pharmacy and Wal-Mart because I saw a credit card charge. She has MS."

"She has MS?" He proceeds to tell me that his partner has MS.

"Look," I said with impatience to redirect the focus, "What can you do? Can you put an APB out for her car? I'm worried. She could have been overpowered by someone in a parking lot. Maybe she was in an accident." I wondered if she might have been in an accident that she purposely caused. I didn't tell the officer this, but the thought crossed my mind.

The officer told me he could play the MS card and get it out there publicly, but he wanted to talk to his sergeant first about how far he should take it. He suggested that he didn't want to involve North Texas resources if it was just a "mommy vacation." They could keep an eye out for the vehicle, but maybe it was too early to mobilize the AMBER Alert system – which would announce it on the news and digital freeway signs. It also seemed like it would become complex, involving levels of decision-makers, paperwork and broadcast alerts across the state. He was fishing. I think he was leaving it to me to tell him to "Do whatever it takes!"

I tried to think. I asked if he could launch an "almost AMBER Alert."

He caught the notion I wasn't committed to the full scale launch and suggested I try Googling some local hospitals or the morgues to see if she was on the manifest. He then gave me his card and left with paperwork under his arm.

I went upstairs to my office and watched him through the window as he took the next ten minutes to enter all the data into his patrol car's computer before he finally drove away.

CHAPTER 15

A Night to Remember
BY CHRIS

I took the officer's advice spending the next hour looking for Nancy online. I'm checking local hospitals, hotels and even morgues. I'm making calls.

I feel fear. My mind is bouncing between trusting God and trying to take control of the situation. I'm uncertain. I am extremely tired.

My head falls forward into slumber, almost falling asleep at my laptop. In one second, I shake my head from the sensation of nodding off. With total consciousness I pull out a short but meaningful prayer from deep within:

"Lord, sustain her life. Keep her alive. Let someone find her," I said aloud.

Then I stand up, walk downstairs to our bedroom, and crash into bed.

When my head hit the pillow, I was so drowsy from the day's emotional roller coaster, I fell right to sleep.

It seemed like immediately I was transported to a pavilion with ground fog. The pavilion was supported with pillars and beams. It was tall but open. There were no walls, but there was a covering overhead. It reminded me of a lunch area we used to have when I was young, at Village Christian School. It was dark, not pitch black, just moody, like the stage before the opening scene lights up the set. I sat alone watching as Nancy entered the pavilion from stage left.

Jesus was facing me and was kneeling down; His hands were busy at work. It seemed like he was preparing something on the floor. I stared closer. He was wrapping gifts. About four, maybe six of them, of various sizes. His arms were busy folding silver paper around a package and reaching for ribbon. Nancy walked over to Him, slowly and a bit shy. She surprised Jesus – who had this expression as if He was wrapping *her* presents and she suddenly walked in on Him. "You're not supposed to be here," Jesus said with a smile. His surprise didn't stir any anger. He was compassionate; tender, even.

He stood up and gently put His arm around her shoulder. He

turned her around and walked her in the other direction, so that she wouldn't see what He was wrapping.

I saw that He started a conversation with Nancy, persuading her with hand gestures, but I could not hear the words. I did, however, know by His nonverbal gestures that He was giving her a choice to either stay or go. His arms and hands moved left and then right again. His expressions seemed to end with a question, waiting on Nancy's answer.

Nancy looked down and then at Him. She looked right into His eyes. She smiled and nodded. She seemed sure.

The dream ended abruptly because I awoke to the phone ringing.

CHAPTER 16

To the Very End and Back

BY CHRIS

7:50 AM, Monday, April 13, 2009

"Hello, who is this?" The first question in my mind was: *Which person is calling me – Nancy, the police, the hospital, the morgue?*

I could hear commotion and voices in the background. "Mr. Conant, we're the paramedics who arrived at the scene and we're with your wife."

"Where is she? What happened?!" I shouted.

"Apparently, sir, she has taken over 90 Xanax pills, 90 Ambien, and a bunch of Vicodin, and we're taking her to Medical Center of Arlington. Could you tell me if she has any allergies to any medications?"

As my mind wakes up I think, *why is this relevant?* Is he asking me if the medications she takes will counteract with another drug? I have no idea. "Um, no, I don't know. Where are you now?"

"We're at the Hampton Inn, but you'll need to meet us at MCA Hospital. She's breathing. We're transporting her now. *She's alive!*"

The words hung on the airwaves like an echo, "She's alive!" I hung up the phone. Then the thought came: *overdose. She finally did it,* I thought coldly.

The girls weren't awake yet. I called Bob Oliver, our pastor and neighbor. Anna, his wife, answered.

"What's wrong?" she asked.

"Nancy overdosed," I paused to swallow the words I just uttered. "I don't have any details except she's alive and she's at Medical Center of Arlington." Anna started crying. I asked, "I know it's your day off, but can I have Bob for a little while? I need to send my girls somewhere today. They're off school." Random thoughts flooded my mind as I immediately transitioned into catatonic autopilot. *I should put the trash out. The dog needs food in her bowl. I need to go see my wife in the hospital. Should I start a load of laundry?*

"I'm sorry, Anna; I'm not thinking clearly, except that I need to see Nancy. Can you send Bob over?"

"Bob will be over in a few minutes."

I got dressed and fed the animals. I went to the front door and looked out the side window. Bob was walking up. I opened the door before Bob could knock.

"Bob," I said, "the girls are still sleeping, so if you could, tell them that their mom is in the hospital and I went to check on her. I'll call them later."

Just then, Bekah came out of her room. So I told her what I had just said to Bob. I played it way down, but I was careful not to lie about it. "I'll give you a call later and let you know how she's doing," I said as I ambled away, trying to act natural and keep it light so she wouldn't worry too much. This was a characteristic of my side of the family. Growing up, we would play down pain, emotion and suffering. I realize there are times when it's healthy to do this and times when it's not. The problem is, I'm so used to playing it down, I don't know when it's okay or inappropriate.

Bekah was used to Mom going into the hospital for exacerbations, so she took it as par-for-the-course. Playing it down worked well this time.

8:20 AM

I arrived at the emergency room and went to the check-in nurse. She was kind and cheerful.

When I told her who I was and who I was there to see, it was like a red flag came up on her monitor because her countenance changed from cheerful to guarded. I felt like I said the wrong word. Or pressed an off-switch.

I had to sign a bunch of papers saying that I would be financially responsible for her care. One of the forms asked if I had a do-not-resuscitate order, which Nancy had told me she put in place a couple of weeks earlier (unbeknownst to me—part of her master plan), but for now I just ignored the question.

I finished the forms in about three minutes and gave them back to the check-in nurse. I asked if I could see Nancy. The nurse said she'd have to investigate and I should take a seat.

After 20 minutes of waiting, I went back to the counter and demanded to talk with someone to find out what had happened.

Another 10 minutes… then a Registered Nurse came out with a police officer. I felt incredibly scared and threatened. *Did he think I was going to get violent?* They both sat down next to me.

The RN started, "Your wife took a lot of prescription medications, which appears to be a suicide attempt. In fact, Mr. Conant, we don't know how many total pills, but we know it was at least 180 from the paramedic reports. Ninety were Xanax. The Xanax alone are enough to kill you, me, and the big guy sitting over there."

This was not a superficial attempt. Nancy was serious. She really wanted to go.

"Have you pumped her stomach out? Or given her some carbon to absorb it?" I had no idea what the right question was, but I knew I just wanted to obtain more detail and keep them talking to me.

The nurse continued, "The doctor is with her, and she is responding incredibly well. It appears that she overdosed more than 12 hours ago. It is really a miracle that she is alive. The quantity she took is, in fact, extremely lethal. We really can't explain how she survived it."

"She is awake, but she is belligerent. She needs a catheter, and she won't let us do it—unless we restrain her."

"Then restrain her if that's what it takes to get her well," I retorted with emphasis. I'm sure it came out very bitter as I switched into a mean "tough love" mode. I was in shock, but deep down, not surprised that Nancy had gone all the way.

It was also the very moment I remembered the dream I had just hours before. It was the first time I considered that she might have died and come back to life.

Starting right there, and for the next few weeks, I would rotate through glad, sad and mad feelings.

My mind wandered. That "belligerent" comment took me back 15 years to when this had happened before.

Yes, before.

Nancy had superficially attempted suicide in 1994, though not in the same way. It was the equivalent to "cutting," a self-harming behavior that teenagers today might try. Nancy had lost her dog of 14 years to cancer. She had trouble coping with the pain. She called me at work to threaten me that she's going to attempt to take her life, so I hung up and called 911 to get an ambulance to rush over. She took a few pills, maybe a dozen. The paramedics found Nancy, on a lawn chair in the backyard, waiting for her "attempt" to take effect. They took her straight to the hospital and placed her on a 72-hour lockdown. Nancy was so mad at me. I visited her in the emergency room in her agitated state. She had superficial cut marks on her arms and liquid black charcoal coming out of her mouth, just having had her stomach pumped. She was seething mad, cussing, and for a couple days, belligerent with anyone who came near her. I reflected on this time when Nancy harbored deep rage against me, against herself, against the world and against God.

This situation was very different. Nancy expected this to be final, so she was probably going to be ornery and possibly confused that she's alive. Alive when she should be dead.

The officer who sat with the nurse told me that Nancy was in custody but not under arrest. Surprisingly, Nancy was coherent enough to have asked him about some letters she had written to us. He told me that her belongings were at the Hampton Inn on Interstate 20. I knew where it was.

I decided that if I couldn't see Nancy, and because she was in the care of others, then I would head over to the Hampton Inn, get some more answers, decide what to do and return to the hospital in a couple of hours.

9:30 AM

I arrived at the Hampton Inn and talked to the desk clerk who had checked Nancy in. Her eyes widened when I introduced myself. She was afraid to talk to me and directed me to the manager. The manager came around the corner, introduced herself and handed me a bag of wet belongings and a stack of letters and cards.

After I asked what had happened, she told me in a soft voice, but straight-up, "Your wife blended a bunch of pills into a smoothie and drank it." The manager was trying to be helpful, but obviously the moment was uncomfortable for both of us.

It's unnatural to have casual conversation about such things.

"Why are all of her belongings wet?" I was puzzled.

She asked me to wait while she called the housekeeper and maintenance guy. Within a minute, it was a group of five of us around the front desk. It was difficult to not feel embarrassment, but I wanted more answers.

Bewildered themselves, they tried to explain how the sink was on and overflowing even though there was nothing wrong with the drain or plugging it. Water had backed up in the sink, overflowed, went down the cabinet and formed a one-inch pool on the floor. The water made its way to the room beneath, where pieces of water-soaked drywall had started falling off the ceiling.

The housekeeper went into the room downstairs for a routine cleaning and saw the wet drywall on the floor. She proceeded to investigate the source. She alerted the manager. They went upstairs and knocked on the door loudly. Nancy answered and beckoned them to come in.

They entered with a master key card, and together they found Nancy lying in the pool of water on the floor. Nancy was "coming to" and asked the manager, "Are you an angel?"

The manager replied "No, oh my gosh!" and looked around the room. The bed was unmade with a circle of pillows on it. The curtains were drawn. An empty blender was on the counter. Pill bottles were empty and arranged in a group. She immediately called the paramedics.

Nancy drifted in and out of consciousness, but she was breathing rapidly, like she had an adrenaline shot. The paramedics arrived and went straight to the room with a stretcher and a large tackle box full of medical supplies. They were able to assess the situation, get an I.V. in Nancy, and stabilize her for transport.

This was getting too uncomfortable for me. I didn't want to hear any more.

I thanked them for taking care of her and left for home with Nancy's belongings. The manager gave me her card and asked me to call her later. She mentioned something about damages.

I called Bob and Anna and said I didn't really know what to do next but I needed to try to talk about it. I wanted to force myself to start processing my feelings.

"The girls are fine and over at Kara's house," Bob said with comforting words. "They can stay there all day if you need."

"I think I need to talk about what's going on. Can you come over?" I hoped.

"Where are you now?"

"I'm on my way home." I replied.

"Sure," Bob offered. "I can come by in an hour." Then he prayed for me over the phone.

When I arrived home, I opened the bag from the hotel. In it were the clothes that Nancy had dressed in for Easter service the day before when we had the argument. I loaded them into the washing machine.

The bag also had a coffee bean grinder and a blender. Instantly, I knew that the blender was the instrument that mixed the death smoothie. The coffee bean grinder still had a trace amount of pill residue in it.

There was a letter to Meghan, to Bekah and one to me. Each letter had a corresponding card.

I started reading my letter. It was more of the same that I'd heard over and over during the previous months: Nancy really wanted to get this life over with and be present with Jesus. She told me that I would be better off with someone else. That I am a good man, good father, and good husband. That it was time for her to go. It was a weave of lies intermixed with sugarcoated loving thoughts. It was a waste of penmanship. My eyes lacked interest and went dull. I knew the lies were literally from Satan, constantly whispered into Nancy's mind so that she would believe them.

I read the letters addressed to Meghan and Rebekah, too. All the letters had a theme like "press on even though I'm gone." It complimented how wonderful and beautiful and amazing they are. *Encouragement,* I thought, *that would fall on deaf ears if Nancy is dead!* How could Nancy think Bekah and Meghan would be so understanding after their Mom took her own life?

I also pulled Nancy's purse, Bible and cell phone out of the bag. I checked her phone and looked at the calls. They were all unanswered calls from me.

I continued to rummage through the belongings. The paramedics told me there were three pill bottles, but there were nine in total. Assuming they were recently filled prescriptions, it would have been 330-450 pills of various sorts, fatally toxic in combinations of just a couple of dozen pills. I stacked them all on our bathroom counter.

Bob rang the doorbell. He came in and sat down. I told him the story of what I knew so far. He listened well, and I felt better after sharing the load that been dropped on me. I still had mixed feelings about the whole ordeal.

Bob prayed for Nancy and I. I thought it best to let our friends Tami McNulty and Heather Harbaugh know so they could be praying for us too, especially since I was heading back to the hospital – this time with Bob.

CHAPTER 17

A Reluctant Visit

BY CHRIS

10:50 AM, Monday, April 13, 2009

Bob and I rode together back to the hospital and located Nancy's room. We found her sitting up on the edge of the bed, in the process of being transferred from the Emergency Room to ICU. I had mixed feelings about being there.

I had not spoken to her since Easter morning, which seemed like forever, but was only 24 hours earlier. My first words were all about coping. I had purposed to be distant to protect my feelings.

"Hey, how are you?" She didn't look up from the wheelchair she was now sitting in. She was groggy, but awake.

I need to point out here that Nancy's emergency room recovery was incredibly rapid. First, she did not need her stomach pumped. After enough medication to kill three men, it's like God just flushed it out of her system with an IV bag. "Unheard of. It's really a miracle," I was told by her emergency room physician. Second, she didn't need to go to ICU on a stretcher. She was standing up and moving from bed to wheelchair. Third, she was alert and responsive compared to her despondency over the prior weeks and months.

They wheeled her to a private room, and I went in by myself. Bob stayed in the waiting room.

"I'm not supposed to be here," Nancy mumbled.

"Who found me?" she questioned.

"Did you get the letters?" she continued.

"What letters?" I wanted to make her say to me that they were her final communication to the three of us, to see if she remembered what she did.

"I wrote you all and said goodbye."

This was the second time I contemplated that maybe she had died and been brought back to life. The amount of pills taken was extensive. It was very final. How could Nancy survive all that and be present with me right now, alive, and asking me these questions?

Something had happened to her. She had "presence." Her countenance was healthy and connected, not despondent. Just three hours earlier she was lying in a pool of water in the hotel room, having overdosed —and now we were having a conversation! My mind flashed back to the dream I had earlier that morning, of her in the presence of Jesus. Was she in Heaven just a few hours earlier?

It was surreal. My emotions were all over the place.

I needed a break, an emotional distance from what I had just experienced. Knowing Nancy was in good care, Bob and I left around 11:15 am.

Looking for something familiar, I went to get the kids. I took them to our favorite restaurant for lunch in our '77 Ford Pickup named Rusty.

I really enjoy spending time with my two girls. Next to Nancy, they are my two, most favorite people in the world. I have told them time and again, they are both incredibly beautiful and intelligent and they each have a bright future in Christ. They have unique characteristics, each finding their own way, but they are on the right track. They have had to face some very grown-up responsibilities very early on, and have matured very quickly as a result.

Bekah is outgoing and has a missionary's heart. She is wired for creativity, communications, organization, business and evangelism. She will prophecy and preach. She is a servant/leader. She is a worshipper. She loves her sister.

Meghan admires her sister, but found the beat to her own drum. She too has business acumen with deep insights with an incredible sense of justice and law. She has a holy aspect to her character, and is set-apart. She is a writer and an athlete. She is a warrior for righteousness.

Whenever I pray for them, I see these traits budding at a young age. I know it's my job as a father to love them and call these qualities forth into being.

The girls and I sat down for a late lunch. Bekah ordered a burger with sweet potato fries. Meghan ordered mac and cheese off the kid's menu. It felt normal for a few moments – except we missed Nancy.

After lunch, Bekah asked, could I visit Mom in the hospital?"

"No, Bekah. The hospital doesn't allow children in the ICU," I explained.

"What's the ICU?" Meghan questioned.

"It's the Intensive Care Unit, where they'll take extra care of Mom, and others who need special care."

"Is she *really* sick?" Bekah inquired.

"The good news is that your Mom is getting better. She's resting now, and they want to monitor her progress as she improves. When she's better you can see her again." It ended the discussion, and after paying the bill, we walked out to the parking lot and climbed into Rusty.

Driving home with the window rolled down, I thought about what it would have been like to explain their Mom's death to them. In my mind I played the scenario:

"Bekah, Meghan, I have some bad news. Your Mom died." No, that's too harsh and abrupt for a young mind. *Try again.*

"Bekah, Meghan, I mentioned that your Mom was out last night. Well, actually, I found out this morning that she passed away. Suddenly."

"How did she die?" Bekah would certainly ask. And right there is when my mind stopped playing *that* game.

Later that evening, our friends Tami, Heather, Bob and Anna went to pray over Nancy in the ICU and sing worship songs to the Lord. They declared God's Word through song over Nancy as she slept off what remained of her Monday ordeal.

CHAPTER 18

In Custody

BY CHRIS

10:30 AM, Tuesday, April 14, 2009

I had already dropped the kids off at school and was busy getting some work done at home. I had already contacted the police the afternoon before to let them know Nancy was found.

Travis, the attending nurse at the hospital, phoned me to report Nancy had made a speedy 24-hour recovery and they were already releasing her to Millwood, a psychiatric facility, at about 1:00 PM.

I asked if she could have anything, like clothes, a notebook or her phone. Travis said "Millwood has restrictions on what patients can bring in, so keep it basic, like pajamas."

I put a suitcase together and drove over to visit Nancy.

I stopped at the nurse's station and spoke with Travis. "Has she been belligerent?" was on the top of my list of questions.

"Belligerent, no. She's been really easy-going. Really cool."

I was wondering if there was manipulation going on. Perhaps Nancy wanted something so she was being nice. I started to walk toward her room.

"Oh," Travis said, "she's still in custody, so you may want to break the news that she has to transfer to Millwood in the back of a police car."

Before I entered the room, I stopped to pray about something very important. I sat down in a chair just outside her room. Here, I had a choice to make. A choice to love or a choice to hate. I could extend grace to Nancy and forgive her. I could stay positive and encouraging. Or, I could justify to myself that I have every right to be angry, bitter, holding her responsible for any future fallout from this event. It was truly a pivotal moment in our relationship. As I prayed, I felt lightened, because I realized God could be trusted. He could sort out the feelings I had and get to the business of rebuilding our marriage in Him. I felt like it would be good. Maybe better than good if I stayed. It was also the very moment when God put five words in my mind that set me perfectly on track to love her. "As I have forgiven you." It meant, I should extend forgiveness to her because He extended the same forgiveness to me for my mess-ups.

I rose to my feet with new-found courage and rounded the corner into her room. Nancy's face was glowing. I asked if she had heard "angels" singing in her room last night, referring to our friends worshipping in her room and praying for her.

I can't say she was her normal self because, recently, her normal self was being resigned that MS had become her identity.

The person in front of me now had a new normal, a "before-she-had-MS" normal. I remember this Nancy. This was "fun" Nancy – the best friend I travelled with on all those Southern California weekend jaunts B.C. (Before Children).

I was in the mood to laugh now, so I asked Nancy, "Why did you blend the pills with a Lemon-Berry Cream Smoothie when everyone knows if you want to "off" yourself, you need to use the Strawberry-Banana?"

Nancy cracked up.

Then with a bewildered expression, she asked me, "How was I found? I mean," she paused to explain, "at 5:00 PM, I drank the mix, turned off my phone, laid down with pillows all around me and went to sleep… forever."

"You don't remember a thing?" I asked.

"Hardly."

"You were lying on the floor," I reported. "The manager found you. Water had been turned on and was inexplicably overflowing out of the sink. The manager said that when she knocked at about 7:30 AM, you responded to her voice and said you were on the floor in a pool of water and couldn't get up. She asked if she could come in and help, and you said, 'Yes.' When she came in, you asked her if she was an angel. The manager saw what was lying around, and she immediately called the paramedics."

"Oh my goodness!" Nancy's eyes were wide with astonishment.

"There's more. You need to be transferred now to Millwood. I found out it's a two-week stay, with ten days mandatory. And one other thing: you'll be taken in a squad car, not an ambulance. You're in custody, Nance."

I left Nancy wanting to come home with me, hidden in the suitcase. Secretly, I wanted that, too.

CHAPTER 19

The Wreckage of My Crash
BY NANCY

About 16 hours had passed since I downed the concoction on Sunday afternoon, and after being admitted to the ER at the hospital, it was the first time I felt fully aware that I was *not* in heaven! I was shocked and downright ornery. *What am I still doing here?! How is this possible? My plan to be in heaven could not fail! I can't believe it! This can't be happening! Did Jesus not want me? Did He reject me? Oh God. I have to face reality! What now?!*

I kept slipping in and out of consciousness, but I was in quite the irritable mood. My initial reaction was to refuse any medical treatment. I wanted to be with Jesus, not in a hospital room getting nursed back to health. Then, strangely, that desire started to subside and a calm began to settle over me.

I vaguely remembered seeing Chris among the visitors when being transferred from ER to ICU. He was holding my hand, and as he faded away, I recalled him saying to me, "I'll see you tomorrow."

I slept most of the day. I remember hearing familiar voices later that night – Bob and Anna (our pastors) and there were women's voices, too – singing and praying over me.

"Are you angels?" I managed to ask. And then I fell asleep again.

The following morning, a Tuesday, I awoke refreshed and a bit at ease. A new nurse was on duty, a male nurse, named Trevor. He was an odd fellow, but had a gentle way about him that immediately disarmed me. I dropped my defenses – just a bit. I still had no memory of any of the events that took place after downing my concoction. I figured out that I was transferred to the ICU because I was on suicide watch, a 72-hour surveillance.

My thoughts turned towards Chris. I couldn't imagine what he was thinking or feeling. I had a sick feeling in the pit of my stomach. What kind of wreckage have I created now? I never expected to be around to deal with it. My mind was whirling with a thousand questions, and there was no one to provide any answers. I felt so alone.

Time moved so slowly, and I had plenty of it to wonder. *How could I still be alive? My plan was supposed to be foolproof.* I was absolutely bewildered. *How could this have failed?* I wished I could remember something – anything – but I could not then, nor to this day, recall the hours between taking the fatal drink and my stay in the Emergency Room. Much of my entire yesterday I could not remember, probably because I slept most of it. However, I do remember feeling at peace.

Chris came to my room with a small suitcase in tow. His mood was… tender and happy. It was easy to love him. He was jolly and making jokes. I couldn't believe anyone could get a smile out of me, let alone a full-on belly laugh!

He explained that they were getting ready to transfer me out of ICU to Millwood.

Oh boy, here we go again, I thought. I was no stranger to the "nut-hut."

Many years ago, before I got married, before I got clean and sober, I had spent several stints confined for incidents such as drug abuse, major depression and attempts to end my life. *I can't believe this is happening. Again.*

Chris ran through the drill in a nonchalant way. "So, the hospital staff said they can't take you in an ambulance. You will have to go with the police."

The words were still lingering in the air. *Go with the police? Am I in custody? Right! I am a danger to myself. Wait – did I do something illegal?* Here again, I never considered this since I did not expect to be here!

Chris continued, "They should be here any time now. I called Millwood and asked what I could pack for you. Basically, everything is contraband, but they do allow PJ's, so I packed a few for you, some socks, undies, and your Bible and journal, too."

Chris lightened the mood. We chatted and joked about the girls and their habits, and then Chris filled me in on some of the details over the past 36 hours. "There were two miracles!" he exclaimed with great enthusiasm. "First, you're alive! The nurse in the ER told me what you ingested would've been enough to kill three adults! And Nancy. Get this. They didn't need to pump your stomach. I think the IV bag was it. No medical intervention. It's as if your system drained the drugs out all on its own. It was weird because it all happened so fast. You are a miracle, Nancy! Right now I should be planning your funeral, but God has other plans for you!"

CHAPTER 20

The Veil Is Lifted

BY NANCY

Not long after Chris disappeared from sight, two police officers appeared at the nurse's station. I could see Trevor talking with them as he looked my way. Moments later we all met at the doorway of my room.

"Is it time?" I asked.

"It's time," Trevor replied.

As one of the officers came up behind me, he started rattling off some bit about, "This is just standard procedure…" and "…if I could just get you to turn around…" Suddenly I felt the cold steel of the handcuffs pressing in on my wrists, already bruised and swollen from the restraints in the ER. Trevor came up close beside me and whispered in my ear, "This is your new beginning. Make the most of it. I want you to come back and tell me how you're doing. Okay?"

He asked the officers to wait as he hurried off to retrieve a hospital gown. He wrapped it around my shoulders to cover the handcuffs behind my back, still whispering words of encouragement in my ear. It was his attempt to cover my shame.

In that moment, a veil lifted off my eyes, and I became aware that Trevor was truly being used as an instrument of the Lord that day. Whether or not Trevor knew or revered the Lord, God used him to speak words of affirmation and encouragement to me. Trevor's action showed me that *God* was covering my shame. I no longer felt alone. I knew my God was with me.

CHAPTER 21

Walking It Out

BY NANCY

The ride in the police car was the longest car ride I've ever taken. It was hot and cramped in the back seat. Because my hands were cuffed behind my back, I was forced to twist into this bizarre, contorted position. Waves of nausea came over me as sweat dripped down my face. *What if a neighbor or another mom from the kids' school pulls up next to the squad car? Wouldn't that just be the icing on the cake!*

We finally arrived at Millwood after what felt like a "forever" ride, but was in fact only a few short miles from the hospital. Both of the officers escorted me, still cuffed and covered with the gown, through the halls of my new place of residence. I fixed my eyes directly on the floor. I let my hair fall over my face in the hope that I would be invisible. I wished I wasn't there. I wished I wasn't anywhere. These were not streets of gold. They're corridors of linoleum tiles! *Oh Lord, walk this path with me.*

119

As I stepped through the sterile, prison-like corridors, words of affirmation entered my mind and became a fountain to my thoughts. I knew His Spirit was speaking to mine and in that moment I sensed renewed strength and peace. His love carried me, and I knew these words were to sustain me for what was yet to come:

I will never leave nor forsake you.

Hebrews 13:5 (NKJV)

Behold, I make all things new.

Revelation 21:5 (KJV)

Upon arrival, Millwood staff put me through what they call an intake procedure. That's the moment you become painfully aware that all your rights have been stripped from you. It's a most undignified and humiliating process. I knew the drill, since I had been through it many times before. After they check the clothing on your body for any dangerous ropes or ties, they pat you down for weapons or drugs. Then they set your suitcase up on the table and begin to remove every item. They make a list of your belongings and create a pile of contraband items. Pretty much everything ends up in that pile.

Chris had been diligent to only pack what they allowed, so when the staff finished their search, they returned nearly all of my belongings to the suitcase and ushered me down the stale corridors to my room. My roommate was sleeping when we entered. The staff frowns upon daytime sleeping, but the intake nurse said nothing to her. She snored – loudly – and I later discovered she often spent time isolated in the room. Fortunately, she did leave the room from time to time, and that afforded me periods of solitude to study and pray.

CHAPTER 22

Girl Interrupted

BY NANCY

The inside of a mental institution is an odd and surreal place. It can be downright frightening. The sites, sounds, even smells can overwhelm the senses. The staffers can be as unusual as the patients. Some use their position to lord over other human beings and appear to get a thrill out of doing so. Others who work at these facilities genuinely want to be there to make a difference. It can't be an easy job, either way.

As I mentioned earlier, I was no stranger to psych hospitals. I had seen the corridors of a dozen facilities. Some were actually quite nice – as nice as such a facility could be. Others were simply despicable. Millwood fell somewhere in between.

In my youth, when I was well-insured, I was afforded a stay at a hospital that felt more like a resort, complete with swimming pool and fully equipped with an exquisite cafeteria and dining hall. They provided games and movies. There were all sorts of interesting, unique people. We would stay up late into the night, talking and laughing over a round of dominos. I didn't take my predicament seriously at all. I was young and foolish.

Later down the road, when the insurance ran out, I was afforded a bed at a County facility. Such facilities seem like hell on earth.

County reminded me of the movie *Girl Interrupted*, with Angelina Jolie and Winona Ryder. I felt a bit like Winona Ryder's character, who had been committed against her will into a disorderly environment. Just like the movie, I was surrounded by absolute chaos. People were being hauled off in straight jackets; others kicked and screamed and were being restrained to their beds; staff ran frantically to intercept a stray soul. I, too, caused my own share of ruckuses when I didn't get the right meds or was displeased in one way or another. The environment was sickening.

In one instance, I was sitting in the cafeteria with a tray of extremely unappealing food in front of me when a man sat down next to me. All he could manage were guttural groans and moans until he finally defecated in his pants and proceed to vomit on his tray.

I've been confined with young and old, men and women, and alongside every type of mental illness known to man. I have a hunch that demonic forces are behind some cases, if not all, frustrating and tormenting people to different degrees. It's a heart-wrenching thing to hear someone crying and wailing because they were sure they were supposed to be released *that* day, only to find out it was *not* their day of liberation, nor would *that* day come for them anytime soon. It's a terribly sad place to be.

However, my stay at Millwood seemed completely different. The surroundings were not the focus, nor did they overwhelm me; the condition of my heart was the focus, and God had my full attention.

In times past, I would either try to isolate or not deal with the issues at hand. This time, when I went to my room to be alone, the staff would find me at the foot of the bed with my Bible and journal, furiously taking notes. They quietly closed the door and let me be. It was a time to listen up! The Lord was speaking to me. Maybe they sensed this and gave me grace.

Speaking of grace, it was all very strange. I was permitted to have visits during off-times, use the doctor's conference area, make telephone calls when I needed, and was afforded a level of extraordinary privileges. The whole stay was surreal in an unusually favorable way: staff, doctors and the other patients treated me differently. Perhaps they saw Christ in me.

I participated in every group activity and mealtime. When it was downtime, and I wasn't engaged in conversation with another patient or praying for someone, I seized the opportunity to get alone with God and engage in prayer and meditation.

My life had been "interrupted" and it was time to reclaim it for God.

CHAPTER 23

Surrender

BY NANCY

I sat on the edge of my bed and began to reflect on the recent events. A deep sense of regret and sorrow – as well as a deep sense of gratitude and a firm resolve to NEVER allow myself to be deceived or compromised again – began to overflow within. *Lord, let this resolve burn deep within my heart all the days of my life. For my life is truly not my own but is Yours to do with as You please.*

Godly sorrow brings repentance that leads to salvation and leaves no regret, but worldly sorrow brings death. See what this Godly sorrow has produced in you: what earnestness, what eagerness to clear yourselves, what indignation, what alarm, what longing, what concern, what readiness to see justice done.

2 Corinthians 7:10-11 (NIV)

Though my heart's desire was to remain in a state of surrender to God and to walk out my faith in a deep and abiding way from this point on, I knew that I would always have to battle the subtle apathy that seeps in after the initial ordeal has passed. How do I remain as passionate tomorrow, next week, a year from now, as I am at this very moment? How do I stay determined?

A friend of mine, named Sally O'Connor, has written many songs. The lyrics in her song below beautifully describe how I will remain surrendered and determined.

Lord live in me
Lord live in me

The only way I will ever be free
Is if You live in me

Make my life a fragrance
Of Your life in mine

A pure and wondrous perfume poured
A sweet and holy wine

Teach my heart to see You
My lips to sing Your praise
Without Your life inside of me
I perish all my days

Lord Live in Me. Words & Music: Sally O'Connor
©Copyright 2008 Improbable People Ministries

Surrendering myself to Him is the way to true freedom. It's not of my own doing, but God in me. And I in Christ.

'Not by might nor by power, but by my Spirit,' says the LORD Almighty.

Zechariah 4:6b (NIV)

CHAPTER 24

Like a Rocket

BY CHRIS

Over the course of the next 48 hours, Nancy had permission to make a few calls, as long as they were ten minutes or less.

We barely had enough time to discuss who should know about her situation. I told her I had to involve our friend Linda Haussermann because I needed her to pick up the girls from school, a job Nancy usually did.

I let Nancy decide how she wanted to handle the conversations – who should know and what I should say. It started as a pretty small group and, until this book was written, has remained a small group.

These ten-minute calls were set aside to take care of business. She needed some things from me; she had to break appointments on her calendar; she wanted to know how the girls were doing.

I remember having some angry feelings and thoughts such as, *how dare you try to manage your affairs through me.* Just a couple of days before, she didn't want to involve me in the decision to take her life, and now she wants me to cancel a doctor's appointment?

The grief of her trying to leave my side started to get to me. Now she needed me, and yet I wanted to avoid her! Under different circumstances I would be slaying dragons for her. *Why were my emotions so hard to shake off?* It was hard because she broke my trust and I was hurting. I had anger, grief and unforgiveness trying to grow like weeds inside my heart. I had to learn how to let go of these to Jesus because they prevented us from moving forward.

I finally had an epiphany: *Wait a minute! Did she actually die and come back? 'Till death do us part. Did her death break our vows? Were our vows now void?* I corrected my thinking as I remembered my prayer in the ICU. *No... wait... she died and came back! That's it! It's extraordinary! God put us both in this place to show each other God's forgiveness, love and reconciliation! We both get a second chance! We get to experience a new life together. It's a gift from God, come to us through Nancy's suffering!* There was no way I was about to let that thought escape me.

During these phone calls, God was showing me something different about Nancy's countenance and tone. He was filling her with a joy that I hadn't seen in her for years. She was on fire for the Lord!

I couldn't even keep up with her. She was making full use of the time to reflect, journal and grow from the experience while I looked on with astonishment. She was telling me that during group sessions she had the opportunity to share the Gospel with others and was praying for other patients. It was so uncharacteristic for Nancy-with-MS that it left me baffled.

Her interaction with the staff and other patients was contagious. She had a tenderness and compassion that had faded long ago. She was outgoing. All who were around her loved her. She poured herself into the Bible, and she met the Lord all over again. He poured Himself into her and through her. She was a new creation.

I became very attracted to her.

If I could describe her experience, it's as if she took off like a rocket.

CHAPTER 25

A Strange But Welcome Change
BY NANCY

Visiting time was the highlight at Millwood. It was a quiet evening in the hospital. The corridors were clear, and people were talking in hushed tones, huddled in small groups in the lounge.

In a phone call earlier that day, Chris said he would come, and I was elated and nervous all at the same time. It was only Thursday. I had been at Millwood a little more than 48 hours. Those hours had been long and lonesome, and I just wanted to be with my family.

From a distance I saw Chris coming through the doors. My heart leapt at the sight of him. I wanted to run into his arms, but I contained my excitement, trying to be sensitive to his state of mind. This was a confusing time in our relationship.

We sat on the floor in the corridor and toggled between small talk and reports of what was happening in each of our lives and with the girls.

In the middle of the conversation, he asked me a very pointed question.

"How do I know you won't try to take your life again?"

I answered, "Because no one could possibly manufacture the love and vision and joy the Lord is pouring into me. And Chris, I don't have to wait to be in Heaven to be with Him. I have that right here and now."

That was it! I expressed in a few words what I had known all along, yet through the storms I had let this truth slip away from me: I didn't have to go somewhere else to be with God to experience my freedom. I could experience Him here. On Earth. God's Kingdom in heaven, though sometimes unseen, is available right here. The same Presence and personal relationship with Jesus, the same freedom, power, healing, joy, whatever I sought in heaven was already here—Jesus already *came to us*. And when Jesus rose and returned to heaven to prepare a place for us, He left his Holy Spirit here on Earth as a deposit (with all of God's qualities and power) until Jesus *returns for us*.

I knew in that moment something had broken off of us, something ancient, and we would never be the same again!

CHAPTER 26

The Truth Has Set Me Free
BY NANCY

Chris' question to me had the potential to place all sorts of fear and doubt in my heart and mind. Could I or would I do this again?

Absolutely not!

I pulled out my journal and started scribbling the goodness that God was putting in my mind to write down:

Thursday evening, April 16, 2009

I *am* a new creature in Christ, and it is not I who live, but He who lives in me. My life is not my own. Even when I try to take it, He still has the power to unwind death and do with my life what He wants. I belong to Him, quite literally. The notion of anything different is simply a lie straight from the pit of hell. I now recognize those lies for what they are; I know what they sound like, and I resolve never to be deceived in that way again.

Therefore, if anyone *is* in Christ, *he is* a new creation; old things have passed away; behold, all things have become new.
2 Corinthians 5:17 (NKJV)

Instead, I will speak out who God is, what God sees in me, who He says I am and cause my mind to be "stayed" – my thoughts fixed – on Him. He is my Rock. He is my Fortress, my Deliverer and my Strength! I don't need to remain a captive – to be a prisoner of war.

I *can* be different. I can move *in the opposite spirit.* I can take contrary action to what the enemy is demanding of me, and I can make the choice to stop the dialogue. I can turn my thoughts to Jesus, His truth, who *can* and will set me free.

I will listen for God's still, small voice and look for the way of escape that He promises to make for those who believe. And without fail, a way of escape will suddenly appear!

He brings to my mind His promises given throughout the Scriptures. Victory, strength and healing become a very real, tangible, outcome. Victory through Christ is mine once again! The Truth has set me free indeed!

The temptations in your life are no different from what others experience. And God is faithful. He will not allow the temptation to be more than you can stand. When you are tempted, he will show you a way out so that you can endure. 1 Corinthians 10:13 (NLT)

Then you will know the Truth and the Truth will set you free. John 8:32 (NIV)

To quote a favorite pastor: "I cannot afford to have a thought in my head about me that is not in His."

I am re-learning that during a spiritual attack I can profess and confess His truths with my mouth and praise the only One who promises abundant life and gives hope. And as I move into action and put into practice those things He has spoken, the darkness scatters and once again I am restored to fellowship with The Father! I can walk in victory over the darkness!

Now I see why the reading of God's Word and declaring Scripture over myself is so essential to my life and my healing. I need to let His words water me so I can live. Live forever.

Jesus says in the Bible that He is the Bread of Life. As I take Him in, consuming His words, it's as if I eat to live. It is something I have to do to nourish my spirit and soul.

And once again, even when the devil attempts to destroy me, the Lord can take what the devil intends for evil and transform it for my good. Because God's marvelous "economy" can reach farther than my own good, I believe a failure can be used for the good of others, too!

My chains fall off! The prison door is blown wide open! And once again, I'm free! What a wonderful Savior we have! Those are truths I can stand firmly upon!

CHAPTER 27

Acceptance With Joy
BY NANCY

As I filled my journal with new revelation, a strange, but welcoming peace and acceptance came over me. It was different, like nothing I had ever experienced in all of my years walking with the Lord.

When I was a baby believer in Jesus, I had read a book called Hinds Feet on High Places. (*Spoiler alert!*) The book is a powerful allegory of a girl's journey of faith. The main character in the story, whose name is Much Afraid, is departing from her Fearing Family and traveling to the High Places of the Chief Shepherd. On her voyage, she is guided by two companions, Sorrow and Suffering. Eventually she reaches her destination; only to find out she's been transformed! She is no longer Much Afraid but is now called Acceptance With Joy.

For the past 25 years, I've been walking with Jesus, running from Jesus, arguing with Jesus, separated from Jesus and back together with Jesus. Yep, Jesus and I have been in relationship in one form or another for quite some time now. It's safe to say that my relationship has not been typical, if there is a "typical" relationship to be had with God. I have wandered into some pretty dark places, yet He has proven time and again that His arm is not too short to save and that He will never leave me nor forsake me. True to His Word, He started something, and He's going to finish it, despite all my wanderings.

…being confident of this, that He who began a good work in you will carry it on to completion until the day of Christ Jesus.

Philippians 1:6 (NIV)

In the same way that Much Afraid transformed to Acceptance with Joy, I have decided to let go of my old name, Burden. I can say with all confidence that I'm well on my way to experiencing the same marvelous transformation in my life by God's amazing grace.

He has made my feet like hinds' feet, And makes me walk on my high places.

Habakkuk 3:19 (NASB)

He makes me as surefooted as a deer, enabling me to stand on mountain heights.

Psalm 18:33 (NLT)

CHAPTER 28

Hope For The Future
BY NANCY

It was the third morning at Millwood when Chris told me to call Heather but didn't tell me why. So I hopped on a ten-minute call and dialed her number. That's when I received an invitation to join Heather and Linda on a trip to Bill Johnson's church in Redding, California!

As I initiated the call, before Heather had a chance to tell me this awesome news, I felt it necessary and appropriate to apologize to her and ask her forgiveness for my actions against all that she had invested in my family and in me. She graciously accepted the apology but insisted that none was in order. Instead, she said something that seemed to come right from the mouth of Christ:

"I'm just so sorry that all these months or years, you felt like you had to carry this alone."

No condemnation.

She then went on to explain that the Lord had revealed to her that her visit with Paul to us the week prior to the suicide was for such a time as this.

I hurried back to my room to write down my thoughts and a new favorite Psalm in my journal.

Friday, April 17, 2009

I am rejoicing in my Lord! Only *in* Christ can one be at the depths of death's door and mere days later find myself rejoicing in the Lord! Only *in Christ!* His assurance that victory over darkness is a reality has given me a joy and peace that can sustain me all the days of my life. This can only come from Him!

Praise be to the Lord my Rock, who trains my hands for war, my fingers for battle.
He is my loving God and my fortress, my stronghold and my deliverer, my shield, in whom I take refuge...
O Lord, what is man that you care for him, the son of man that you think of him?
Man is like a breath; his days are like a fleeting shadow.
Part your heavens, O Lord, and come down; touch the mountains, so that they smoke.
Send forth lightning and scatter; shoot your arrows and rout them.

…Reach down your hand from on high; deliver me and rescue me from the mighty waters…

…I will sing a new song to you, O God…

…our daughters will be like pillars carved to adorn a palace.

Our barns will be filled with every kind of provision. Our sheep will increase by thousands, by tens of thousands in our fields; our oxen will draw heavy loads.

There will be no breaching of walls, no going into captivity, no cry of distress in our streets.

Blessed are the people of whom this is true; blessed are the people whose God is the Lord.

Psalm 144 (NIV)

He truly has scattered the enemy of my soul and lead me out of captivity. He is my strength and my refuge and in Him alone, I will put my trust.

CHAPTER 29

Joyous News
BY NANCY

After I wrote down that Psalm in my journal, I came to a very deep realization: I do not live for myself, rather, I live for Him who gives me every breath I take.

Do you not know that your body is the temple of the Holy Spirit who is in you; whom you have from God, and you are not your own? For you were bought with a price, therefore glorify God in your body and in your spirit, which are God's.
1 Corinthians 6:19 (NIV)

Wow, I thought, *I'm not my own!* This realization hit me like a ton of bricks. I wouldn't be writing this had He not intervened in more ways than one. *I wouldn't even be alive* had He not intervened. That realization changed everything. I am His. He bought me when His Son's death became a substitution for mine. He raised me from the dead. I am His and He is mine.

I began to worship and pray Psalm 144 back to God, "Blessed be the Lord my Rock… Who trains my hands for war and my fingers for battle…my Lovingkindness…my Shield…my Refuge… Who rescues me and delivers me out of the flood. I will sing a new song unto my Lord…songs of mercy…songs of deliverance…that our daughters may be pillars sculptured in palatial style. Happy and blessed are the people whose God is the Lord!"

My spontaneous singing was interrupted when one of the hospital staff called me out of my room to interview me – for an *exit* interview. The doctor had decided to release me.

In light of all the wreckage that occurred before Resurrection Monday, it might seem as if the thought of returning home should have struck terror in my heart. However, I was no longer seeing things through the natural lenses of worry. God had given me new vision and insight.

The news of my release only brought unspeakable joy to my heart.

I was going home.

CHAPTER 30

Homecoming
BY CHRIS

After almost three days (about 68 hours) at Millwood, Nancy was released – eleven days ahead of schedule and seven days ahead of what I was told was mandatory.

I drove to Millwood with the girls. As I pulled up, Nancy was outside on a bench with an attendant. Next to her was a suitcase. She was glowing, like Moses, when he spent all that time on the mountaintop with God. She was so delighted to see us. And we were happy to receive her.

While driving home we held hands.

After a tragic event the Sunday before, she was home with us by Friday. It was just so… nice.

I remember thinking about how I *did not* want to return to the way things had been. I couldn't revert to the old ways. I couldn't do "it" again… implying watching Nancy believe lies about herself and all that entailed. I couldn't go there with her, and I couldn't entertain *my* old ways either.

I thought again about our marriage vows and the moment of choice I had at the hospital. I didn't want to look for a loophole out of the marriage. No, I firmly decided *we would miss the blessing*, the very purpose of Christ coming to earth: to reconcile our hearts with God and with one another. We would miss all of it if either of us bailed on our marriage. I am glad that I was forced to choose. I want all of the depth of that powerful transformation. I'm cool with the fact that we're imperfect people—God can do a lot with imperfect people. I want to experience God perfecting our love in our marriage. Through forgiveness. Through healing. Through humility. It was time to experience the kind of reconciliation that only God could bring about.

In my heart I renewed my commitment to Nancy.

And then I said to her, "What attracted me most to you when we dated was how intensely you worshiped God. It was irresistible to me, and I think deep down I wanted a spouse that would 'press in' to God as intensely as I hoped I would. I need positive words, God's Word, to be in our minds, transforming us. Please, decide to pursue God's heart and mind again in our marriage, and our love will never run dry. God will show up. I can't function if you return to the old Nancy, trying to 'escape this world' and rationalizing that you're a burden and we're better off without you."

"I will. It's time. The Lord is making some big changes." Nancy said. Words that were music to my ears, coming from her.

I needed to heed my own words, too. The transformation of a mind, renewed by worshiping God and reading the Word, applied to me as much as it did to her.

That evening, while I had a moment to journal, God showed me something that would later help us in our marriage relationship. I pictured a pyramid in my mind. Christ, or I could interchange God, was at the top, and Nancy was in the bottom left corner, and I was in the bottom right corner. Prior to Resurrection Monday, we had unsuccessfully tried to commit to each other on the strength of our love for each other, at the base of the pyramid, as so many couples do. This failed us.

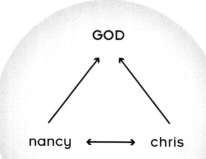

We thought the relationship between us would work,
until we realized that pursuing the bond between Nancy and I
fostered self-reliance, co-dependence, high spiritual expectations
on each other and it sapped our strength.

Now we saw clearly—that there was one path for us. One way. We each had to press into God, toward the peak of the pyramid, hearing His words, drawing closer to Him, letting Him tell us who we are in Christ, and then with hardly any additional effort, we'd certainly discover each other in Him, as we meet together at the apex.

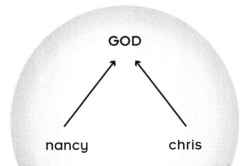

This relationship model may seem simple,
but it's better. Our focus toward God draws us closer together in love
the more we pursue Him. Nancy becomes more attractive to me.
We find joy. Our needs are met by God.

If we are both seeking God, then we inevitably get closer as husband and wife. If our kids seek Him too, then our family inevitably becomes closer. It's probably a simple concept, but for me it was a revelation to redirect my life, especially as a husband and father. It got me excited about the next 50 years with Nancy. He will cause everything to work out for good when we meet *in* Christ. Outside of Him, it won't work. *In* Christ, we grow, we mature, we have revelation, perspective and love.

If Nancy and I both did this, it would be a total "win."

CHAPTER 31

Resurrection Monday

BY CHRIS

Medically, Nancy is a living miracle. She experienced the resurrection power of Christ prevailing in her life. In fact, as final as suicide usually is, we rejoice that Death could not take her for good.

I had many questions about what happened the day Nancy took her life. By the events and signs I experienced, I resolved in my mind that God brought her back from the dead. There was a physical resurrection. Even if I was a skeptic about this, then at the very least I could not deny that her resurrection was also emotional and spiritual.

However, I truly believe God brought her back from death to continue her life here on earth. I believe He received her in heaven, talked with her, let her choose, showed her who she was destined to be, and then sent her back in physical body to a flooded floor in a room overflowing with water (a symbol of baptism and new life). In the three days that followed at Millwood, God spoke to Nancy

in powerful and supernatural ways, just like He spoke to Saul of
Tarsus, attracting Nancy into a complete, magnificent truth about
His love for her.

Through the course of our personal history, vivid dreams, supernatural events, and inexplicable occurrences I witnessed God unfold
the truth that He can work out all things for His good for those
who are *in* Christ.

Too many coincidences happened for these events to be called anything less than a miracle. This was God's providence in Nancy's life.

It is now our very hard and beautiful story to tell.

I can attest that after four years since that hard and beautiful
week, Nancy is consistently in the Word, pursuing God, praying
for me, her children, and praying over others who need a real
healing miracle.

She has insight, inner strength, confidence and joy. She ministers to
others.

Her new name is Overcoming One. Prayer Warrior. One Who
Seeks His Face. Faithful. Lover of God. Healed in Christ. Saved by
God.

She is also my delight, my love and my best friend.

CHAPTER 32

The Gifts That Jesus was Wrapping

BY CHRIS

Jesus was wrapping some gifts when I saw Him, in my dream, surprised by Nancy's approach on Resurrection Monday. Two of those gifts cause me to think of our daughters, Rebekah and Meghan, who have been uniquely placed in Nancy's and my life by God for a special, beautiful purpose.

God also did a wonderful work just days after her return home. After a couple years of taking painting classes, Nancy's artistic talent became masterful and prolific.

God blessed Nancy's hands to create beautiful works. It was an immediate increase in knowledge and skill. It's such an encouragement knowing God can impart such a gift at a later stage of life.

Now, four years later, Nancy has won national awards for her artwork, and painted works for private collections and art auctions, but she has never lost her confidence in Christ. She has been able to travel and attend workshops with pastel masters like June Holloway, Sally Strand and Lesley Harrison. Here is a painting Nancy created at Lesley's workshop called "The Stallion." More of Nancy's work can be seen at www.nancyconant.com

©2012 Nancy Conant

In fact, her paintings are touching others too. At the time of this writing, her Facebook page is approaching 20,000 fans and growing, and the comments from all over the world are a great encouragement to Nancy. On many occasions she has been able to inspire others toward God and His plan for their life.

"I have MS, and you've inspired me to paint again."

"Your paintings look so photographic and real, how do you do it?"

"God has truly given you a gift."

With every question on Facebook comes an opportunity to share a piece of Nancy's hard and beautiful story, which does not stop with a Resurrection. It continues with power, like a magnification of God's awesomeness through her tradecraft!

Nancy will be the first to tell you that she considers painting an act of worship. It's an opportunity for her to demonstrate her love to God by using the gift He gave her...to honor Him right back!

I believe another gift she received is healing. The MS has already been touched by her experience with God that early spring morning on Resurrection Monday. Although not completely healed yet, Nancy is walking again, no longer forced into a wheelchair or on a cane. She's in water aerobics three days a week. Her cognitive function has greatly improved.

Join with me in prayer for her entire abdominal area to be healed. Pray that her MS is 100% gone, her balance restored, and that she would continue to inspire others with her testimony.

While her family, her love of animals and magnificent artwork are sources of pleasure, and the Lord is bringing her tremendous joy through them, I know for certain that her constant source of joy is *in* Christ, because when He met her in those deep dark places, it changed her forever.

I had a strong mental picture of Nancy lying in a casket, and had she remained dead, I would have gone through the motions of planning her funeral, but instead I renewed my marriage vows in my heart. We'll definitely be sealing this commitment with a ceremony. So what the enemy intended to be a funeral, God redeems into a wedding! Isn't that just like our God? To take something broken or used, and give it a renewed purpose?

If we pursue God, we can know Him and what His special plan is for us. I mean, even if circumstances seem hopeless, I'm encouraged! By observing Nancy's life, there is a deep and peaceful joy knowing that not even death will stop God's love and His plan for our life.

That's my King. I feel so blessed and grateful that my wife is a living testimony of His powerful love. I have witnessed first-hand the resurrecting, transforming and healing power of Christ.

God's love is not limited to our family. It is free and available to *anyone* who asks Him for it. If this book encourages you and you would like to know about God's love, we want to show you. If you already know that love but you need to be refreshed in it, either way, please read on and make a commitment toward pursuing God. Nothing in this life tastes, feels, is, so Good.

CHAPTER 33

Hindsight
BY NANCY

Almost four years have passed since Resurrection Monday.
I'm glad to report that the changes the Lord made in my heart
during that time have become a deep and abiding part of me.

My life will never be the same. Neither will my relationship
with the Lord. There has developed a dependence and closeness
that only He could create. I seek Him in all things and have
seen the fruit of His Holy Spirit like never before. For that I am
eternally grateful.

Many of the life lessons I learned around Easter 2009 have
carried me through great challenges and difficulties. I'm pleased
to report I do not continue to entertain the enemy's lies nor buy
into them. My cup runs over with joy. I now know the truth,
and the truth has set me free.

I don't really have much to say about MS. Though there has

been much improvement, there are still signs of the disease present. It is considerably less than what I used to have to deal with, so I know God is at work.

Ultimately, MS doesn't drive my decisions anymore; it carries about as much importance to me as washing dishes. It's there every day, but I don't dwell on it. I used to be distracted by MS like it was an issue routinely in my face. Now God has all my attention and I feel like my focus is always on Him, and the MS has to take a back seat. I believe this perspective has ushered in God's healing in my life.

I think about worship, not beating MS. I think about praying for others, not what I can't do. I write about the positive thoughts and insights God is speaking into my mind through reading the Bible, not taking notes on what the latest advances in MS are. I am free because my identity is not MS. My identity is *in* Christ.

I am well-covered in prayer by our current Gateway Church Grand Prairie family, as well as previous church families where we have spent long seasons of our lives, and I am pursuing Christ in community with others.

I'm free to love life and love those whom the Lord has brought into my life. Our wonderful Bible-believing and Bible-teaching church challenges me to grow in Christ – and to listen to and to obey His words! I never have to be alone. They truly are my family.

Pat Nolan and the Dream Fund introduced me to whole chiropractic care and it has provided relief. I am pursuing wholeness as I pursue Christ.

My beloved husband and best friend, Chris, and I have never been closer. We enjoy a fresh and free love that is built on our pursuit of Christ. We have mutual respect and trust – despite all that's happened in the past. The Lord took us to a new level in our love.

To this day, when I reflect on the cost of my actions, I am overwhelmed. The monetary costs – medical expenses, repairing the damage to the hotel – were in the tens of thousands. Besides the monetary costs, the mental and emotional price Chris paid was immeasurable: the fear, grief, stress and anger, which he never got to fully process until many months later; his loss of work time; pulling focus away from his client responsibilities, putting our business at risk; having to hold things together at home while trying to maintain a stable environment for the children, was a drain beyond description. He handled the whole episode with incredible integrity because he pursued his needs in Christ.

Concerning the money, we both reflected on the two $100 gifts that we had received prior to Resurrection Monday and considered those to be a sign that the Lord would cover the costs. And He did! He provided every penny to repair the two hotel rooms at the Hampton Inn that had been destroyed due to the overflow in my room as well as all the medical expenses not covered by insurance. Through God's provision in the form of an unexpected check, He paid the debt.

I owe a deep debt of gratitude to my husband, who helped me clean up the wreckage of my crash without heaping shame on me. He handled my recovery and story in a way that preserved my dignity. He loved me.

I am so overwhelmed by the kindness and generosity of our Lord, who gave freely and provided our every need.

Chris and I also realize we now have a responsibility and a ministry around our story and we are always submitting the timing and plans to the Lord around how he wants to use it in the lives of others.

The girls were shielded from what happened, and for that I am grateful. At the time, they were too young to process any of it. Since then, my children learned about my story shortly before the publishing of this book. Now that they are older, they have been able to understand and witness that living *in Christ* is a reality. They are strong young women of God who know that reading His Word, knowing His voice and following after Him is life-changing and life-giving.

I cannot emphasize enough the importance of getting close to Christ. I have some information about how to do this in the next chapter.

And if you are eager to read more, we have a short story online in a bonus chapter. You can access it via: nancyconant.com/books/resurrection-monday-bonus/

I learned a very profound truth about endings. They are usually so final. However, *in Christ,* there is no end to His love and how far He's willing to go to save a life.

(Not) The End.

CHAPTER 34

How to Know Jesus, The Savior
BY NANCY

Chris and I are delighted you chose to read our very hard but beautiful story. It has been a labor of love for sure. God first gave me the idea for the book while I was at Millwood. He specifically told me to keep a journal and write all that He did in a book. And now the book is here! It's been a kind of birthing process and I'm relieved after all the labor this baby is finally born!

So much revelation from God came out of those three days at Millwood that I could not contain it in these pages. My excitement for God overflows for you.

Speaking of God, Chris and I would like to ask if the book moved you to trust Him more? We hope so. Whether you have been following Jesus for years, or you have never met Him, we want to bring this refreshing Good News:

God loves you.

He cares about the details in your life.

He wants to heal you.

He wants to set you free from whatever holds you back.

He has an awesome plan for your life.

He cares no matter your age or condition.

He truly loves you.

How can you connect with Jesus and hear His voice?

To know Jesus is to know your true condition before God. Our default condition before God is that we are all, initially, separated from Him and on our own destructive path, called "sin." Life may seem impossible, and you're trying to manage it with an addiction or an unsocial behavior. That's because sometimes sin is easy to spot, like sexual sin, or drugs, or cheating or lying. Sometimes it creeps into our lives subtly, as we try to control our circumstances. It could look like unforgiveness (toward others but also ourselves), selfishness or self-pity. The problem with sin is it keeps growing until it becomes spiritual, emotional and even physical death.

The Bible says that all men – and women – have sinned and fall short of the glory of God and of how Holy (and pure) He is. It also says that the wages of sin (what our sin has earned us, the penalty for sin) is death.

Have you ever sinned? Well, think about if you could answer

"yes" to just one of these questions: Have I ever told a lie? Have I ever taken something that doesn't belong to me? Have I ever had a hateful or impure thought? Have I ever disobeyed my parents? Have I ever become so incredibly despondent that I made agreements with a lying enemy? Have I ever contemplated or tried cutting or attempted suicide? Have I used illicit drugs or abused alcohol to escape from reality? Have I ignored God and tried to build a life of my own choosing?

Knowing Jesus means you resolve that He alone is the answer to the consequence of sin. When He died on that cross, He willingly became a substitute for the death we deserve for the sinful choices we make.

He substituted His sinless life in exchange for our sinful one, and then offered the beautiful gift of eternal life, and a better plan to continue the one we have now if we would simply believe in Him. Please realize this.

He saves us from ourselves.
He saves us from sin.
He saves us from being lost.
He saves us from mental and physical illness.
He saves us from death.

We are all in need of a Savior.

Chris and I would like to introduce you personally to our loving, kind Savior. Allow us to encourage you to pray to Him. If you need help with the words, you can say something like this to Him:

"Jesus, I know that I sin and I am in need of a Savior. I understand that You are the only provision that has been made for me to get out of the destructive ways I live and out from under the enemy's lies. I need You. I need Your healing. Whether I've known of You before, or I'm meeting You for the first time now, I receive You as my Lord and Savior, by surrendering my life to You. Please help me to understand Your love for me. Put Your Word in me. I want to follow You all the days of my life. Amen."

Welcome to God's family!

Tell a Christian friend that you prayed this…they've probably been praying for you!

If you made a decision today to either renew an old commitment to Jesus or make a brand new commitment to Him, we would love to hear from you.

We have a few ways you can reach us and interact.

You can go online and leave us your email with the bonus chapter at nancyconant.com/books/resurrection-monday-bonus

If you prefer to write us a letter, please send it to

Chris and Nancy Conant
Resurrection Monday Ministries
1420 High Pointe Lane
Cedar Hill, TX 75104

If you are on Facebook, you can leave comments on:
www.facebook.com/resurrectionmonday

You may also interact and view Nancy's artwork on her Facebook
page at: www.facebook.com/nancyconantpaintedportraits

If you purchased your book online, such as Amazon.com, you
can log in and leave us a comment and a rating where you
bought it. We want to hear from you.

Thank you for reading our story. May God bless you.

Resources

If you have a medical emergency, dial 911 in the USA for emergency services.

SUICIDE PREVENTION SERVICES

National Suicide Prevention Hotline: 1-800-273-8255

U.S. Veterans Suicide Prevention Hotline is available at: 1-800-273-8255 (Press "1")

The Boys Town National Hotline is a toll free number available to kids, teens and young adults at anytime. They can provide help and hope if you call: 1-800-448-3000
Online: suicidepreventionlifeline.org

International: Contact your local police department or hospital

CHRISTIAN COUNSELING SERVICES

Focus on the Family: 1-800-A-FAMILY (232-6459)
M-F 6am – 8pm MST

Hope for the Heart – June Heart: 1-800-488-HOPE (4673)
M-F 7am – 1am CST

RESOURCES

Family Talk Today – Dr. James Dobson: 1-877-732-6825
Phone lines open 24/7

National Association of Nouthetic Counselors
www.nanc.org/Find-a-Counselor

MS SERVICES

National Multiple Sclerosis Society NMSS: 800 344-4867
www.nationalmssociety.org

WORSHIP MUSIC

Bethel Music: bethelmusic.com

Sally Klein O'Connor, Improbable People Ministries:
www.improbablepeople.org

The organizations on this partial list of resources are not affiliated with
Resurrection Monday. This list does not constitute an endorsement of the
book nor any other resource listed above.

Additional Resources can be found online at
nancyconant.com/books/resurrection-monday-bonus

If you enjoyed Resurrection Monday, you may also like:

Resurrection Monday Devotional

Available 2014

Nancy and Chris reveal more of their story through Scriptural principles and truths you or your group can apply. This simple devotional accompanies the book, Resurrection Monday.

Behold Your Bride

Available Fall 2014

This is the prequel to Resurrection Monday. The early years. The stories before the story. God loves us and He's in the business of crazy miracles. Our family seems to never be in short supply.